WHAT

WE

~~DON'T~~

DO

Advance Praise for *What We Don't Do*

"We have far more power to help those in need than we realize, and *What We Don't Do* is a refreshing and necessary reminder on our ability and responsibility to use that power wisely."

—Moby, musician and author of
Porcelain and *Then It Fell Apart*

"*What We Don't Do* confronts our tendency towards feel-good, surface-level altruism and instead challenges us to upskill in driving social change by embracing discomfort and sacrifice at a level akin to high-performing athletes, doctors, or investors. Clearly written and thoughtfully argued, Cooney inspires readers to take an unflinching look at our failure to reduce the suffering of others, and to translate our values into transformational action."

—David Goldberg, Co-Founder
and CEO, Founders Pledge

"The author issues a challenging call to action to overcome our genetic evolution and our biases that lead to complacent inaction and become more impactful and ethical philanthropists. The self-sacrifice for which he advocates will be both difficult to hear and hard to achieve for most, but this book will hopefully push all of us to do much more to reduce suffering in our world."

—John M. Sobrato, Businessman and Giving Pledge Signatory

"When it comes to eating healthy, it's the things we fail to do (like eating our vegetables) that can lead to the most harm. The same holds true for living an ethical life, as *What We Don't Do* so convincingly argues."

—Dr. Michael Greger, *New York Times* Bestselling author of *How Not to Die*

"This book by Nick Cooney delivers a deep dive into waters often given only a glancing touch. Revealed is the vast space of undone acts that could alleviate extreme suffering—the tradeoffs vs win-wins, going beyond evolutionary psychologies and economic pragmatism to ethics that matters. Hopefully this message will spread through and beyond its readers to make the world healthier and safer for current generations and many thereafter."

—Dr. George Church, Co-Founder of Harvard University's Wyss Institute and *Time* magazine's "100 most influential people in the world" honoree

WHAT WE ~~DON'T~~ DO

Inaction in the Face of Suffering
and the Drive to Do More

NICK COONEY

A REGALO PRESS BOOK
ISBN: 979-8-88845-534-0
ISBN (eBook): 979-8-88845-535-7

What We Don't Do:
Inaction in the Face of Suffering and the Drive to Do More
© 2025 by Nick Cooney
All Rights Reserved

Cover Design by Jim Villaflores

Publishing Team:
Founder and Publisher – Gretchen Young
Editor – Caitlyn Limbaugh
Editorial Assistant – Caitlyn Limbaugh
Managing Editor – Aleigha Kely
Production Manager – Alana Mills
Production Editor – Rachel Paul
Associate Production Manager – Kate Harris

This book, as well as any other Regalo Press publications, may be purchased in bulk quantities at a special discounted rate. Contact orders@regalopress.com for more information.

This is a work of nonfiction. All people, locations, events, and situations are portrayed to the best of the author's memory.

Regalo Press
New York • Nashville
regalopress.com

Published in the United States of America
1 2 3 4 5 6 7 8 9 10

WITH GRATITUDE

To my parents Bill and Pat, for their beliefs, personalities, genes and parenting, without whom and which this book (and of course I) wouldn't exist; and to my parents-in-law Gina and Peter for their great kindness and support.

To my partner Laura, for the love and companionship without which life would be far less happy and fun, and for graciously tolerating me spending a portion of several vacations writing this book.

To those who have donated so generously toward charitable efforts I have been involved with, for bringing into reality our shared goal of effectively helping those in great need.

To the couple dozen people who have been particularly valuable models for me to follow and learn from, and whose actions or words helped steer my own time, money and energy down more productive paths for reducing suffering in the world.

"A person may cause evil to others not only by his actions but by his inaction, and in either case he is justly accountable to them for the injury."
—JOHN STUART MILL

CONTENTS

INTRODUCTION

The idea presented in this book is not a new one. It's been touched on by philosophers and religious leaders intermittently for the past several thousand years. There are a few contemporary books that brush up against the idea as well—sometimes elegantly and persuasively and sometimes with derision. But there is no contemporary book focused squarely on the idea itself. And it is an idea so logical and important in its real-world consequences that it deserves a book of its own.

The idea is also a much-needed one, as it is glaringly absent from contemporary discussions around right and wrong, around social justice and the "isms," around personal responsibility and religious values. In this era of heightened debate over various social issues, and increased attempts to signal beliefs by individuals and corporations alike, it brings a wide-lens view that adds new perspective to these public dialogues.

That said, this idea is not easy to swallow. The main premise may ring true, perhaps so much so that it sounds trite and obvious. But what that premise leads to when we think it through to its logical conclusions is not obvious, and living out the idea (as best we can) requires mental discipline, self-sacrifice, and significant change. Our natural instinct when faced with conclusions that would require such things is to rationalize, to search for reasons to discount or ignore those conclusions—however logical they may be, and even when they flow from an idea we profess to believe.

This is a book about an idea that has been around for ages but is largely unmentioned today. It is an idea that is both obvious and alien, one casually endorsed in theory and consistently ignored in practice.

It is a book about what we don't do. It is about the good things that we could be doing but are not. It is a book about our failures to act and the suffering others will endure as a result.

While this was not the case for most of human history (and still is not true for some people today), for you and me, the good things we *don't* do lead to far more suffering in the world than any directly harmful we *do* do. Our biggest ethical failings are failings of inaction.

But this book is not meant as a downer. Quite the opposite. Because the flip side of the coin is this: in the space of what we haven't done yet sits the opportunity to have tremendous impact on the lives of others. We have far more power to help others, to lessen the suffering in the world around us, than we thought we had. That power lies waiting in what we don't yet do.

PART I

INACTION IN THE FACE OF SUFFERING

CHAPTER ONE

The Baron,
the Sophomore,
and the Savior

*"The worst sin towards our fellow
creatures is not to hate them, but
to be indifferent to them; that's
the essence of inhumanity."*
—GEORGE BERNARD SHAW

Tristerne, France, 1512

There are a few ways to start; one is with a fictional historical anecdote.

The year is 1512 and the setting is a small village called Tristerne in the south of France. The village is home to a large number of very low-income subsistence farmers and a handful of wealthy merchants and barons who had retired to the region, known for its beautiful pastures and warm climate, after careers in Paris.

One such person was a baron named John Pierre, a man who had reached the ripe old age (for his time) of sixty-three and lived in a castle on the outskirts of the village with his wife, several children, and numerous grandchildren. By all accounts John was a good person. He was kind and loving to his family. He was a religious man who attended church weekly and did his best to avoid the cardinal sins of gluttony, lust, jealousy, and so on. Throughout his career, he had been fair in his business dealings. He also was a charitable man who would occasionally give to the poor, assist with the repair and upkeep of the church building, and provide patronage to artists in the village.

In normal circumstances, the subsistence farmers of Tristerne were able to make do with what they had, but occasionally periods of extreme weather wreaked havoc on their livelihoods and food supply. The year 1512 saw a particularly devastating summer drought followed by a prolonged period of intense rain, which together wiped out much of the grain crop that the farmers and their families relied on. By the time winter arrived in the town, so too did a battle with starvation for many of the farming families.

By the end of December, thirty of Tristerne's ten thousand citizens had died of starvation. By January, that number climbed to one hundred fifty. By the end of February, it had jumped still higher to almost two hundred fifty. Starving peasants shuffled into the middle of the town to beg for food or money; some even banged on the doors of John Pierre and the other wealthy merchants and barons in the town, desperate for help.

While John Pierre would occasionally provide a small coin or a loaf of bread, he generally viewed the peasants' problems as their own, not his, responsibility. It's true he had the ability to help them at relatively little cost to himself and his family—he had significant stores of grain and other foods, and considerable wealth—but in his view, he had earned that wealth through honest and hard work, and his duty was to his family and church. By the end of the winter, nearly five hundred people in the village had died from starvation or related diseases.

Three years later, John Pierre himself died a natural death. His funeral service was well attended by extended family, friends, and old business associates, each of whom recounted how good a person he was. His wife spoke about how loving he had been as a husband. His children spoke about how much he had loved them as a father and the lessons he'd taught them. Those who had worked for him spoke of how he had provided them and their families with a decent life. And members of his church spoke about his tireless support for the church building's upkeep and his donations to their charitable relief efforts. The picture they painted was clear: this was a good, ethical person who now lay in repose.

Sitting here with the objectivity that comes from being far removed in space and time from Tristerne in 1512, and having no personal relationship with him, what do you think of John Pierre? More specifically, do you think he lived a good, ethical life?

That description wouldn't sit right with me, and I imagine it wouldn't sit right with you either. Because while John Pierre may have been kind to his family and honest in his business dealings, while he may have engaged in good deeds and avoided doing active harm to others, it is hard to overlook the fact that he had the ability to help those in great need and failed to do so. It is hard to overlook the fact that dozens of people died because he withheld aid he easily could have given. The consequences of John's inaction—suffering and death for many individuals—casts a dark shadow over everything else.

The biggest impact John Pierre had on the lives of those around him was not in the good he did for others. It was not in his refraining from commonplace bad deeds, such as fraud, violence, emotional cruelty, even murder. The biggest impact John Pierre had on the lives of others came from the good things he could have done but chose not to do.

What are the implications of that? And just how similar or dissimilar from John Pierre's life is our own?

Hempstead, New York, 2000

Another way to start is with a personal story.

When I was nineteen and in the first half of my sophomore year of college, I began to think that the cost of renting a dorm room—$1,800 per semester—was hard to justify. It seemed like an exorbitantly high amount of money to me at the time. I was young and had never had that amount of money in the bank, and the cost was being covered by a student loan I would eventually have to pay back. I had a scholarship that covered tuition, so the cost of a dorm room wasn't a marginal addition to a much larger tuition bill. It was my main cost of living at the time.

But frugality wasn't the main reason that the rent payment troubled me. A large number of people had less money to live on in an entire year than I was spending for one semester of a dorm room. Over a billion people live in what international aid organizations term "extreme poverty," currently defined as those living on less than $2.50 per day or around $913 per year. How could I justify dropping $1,800 on a few months use of a desk and a twin bed when there were people starving to death and in extreme poverty in other parts of the world?

So, as the second semester approached, I opted out of getting a dorm room for myself and made plans to spend that semester crashing in friends' rooms. And that's exactly what I did, in addition to spending a number of nights on the couch of the college newspaper where I worked, some in the cubicle of a student activist group I belonged to, and a few on the floor of a large handicapped bathroom on the second floor of the student center—which actually wasn't as bad as it sounds. On the upside, the school's janitors were pretty friendly and rarely said anything when they came in to clean some of these rooms and found me sleeping there. On the downside, spending five nights a week sleeping on the floor of a friend's postage-size dorm room is not a good way to maintain a friendship. At any rate, that is how I spent my second semester, and while at times inconvenient, it wasn't a real hardship.

I'm not sharing this story because I think it's particularly interesting. It also wasn't a very consequential decision since the people I had in mind that were starving or in extreme poverty benefited nothing from my decidedly unheroic sacrifice. I didn't send $1,800 their way. Instead, I just didn't spend the money. A charitable interpretation of my decision would be that I had a good intention but hadn't thought through the lack of real-world impact. Another and more accurate way to interpret it would be that it was a decision made from a focus on personal purity—doing what seemed to be "the right thing"—rather than on outcome. Both literally and metaphorically, it was a sophomoric stab at trying to live ethically.

So, why am I sharing the story? I'm sharing the story because of a conversation that decision generated.

After I opted out of housing for that second semester, my parents were concerned with my plan. When they couldn't persuade me to change my mind, they reached out to the school for help. The Director of Student Affairs, in turn, reached out and arranged for me to meet with her one afternoon.

As we sat face to face in the predictably drab, fluorescent-lit college administrator's office, I explained to the director my reason for passing on a dorm room. It just didn't seem right to be spending that much on a dorm room for a few months when there were people in such extreme poverty, given that I could pretty easily crash on the floor of friends' rooms instead.

She wasn't buying it. After beating around the bush for a while, the director eventually made clear what she thought was going on: I was planning to kill myself. A lot of people that are planning suicide give away their possessions first, she noted, and what I was doing had all the hallmarks of that. When I realized that was her concern, I nearly laughed out loud. I assured her that wasn't the case and that I wasn't even giving away my possessions (unless you count a dorm room as a possession). By the end of the meeting, I think she believed me.

The point of the story is this: to a perfectly average university administrator, it simply wasn't believable that considerations of those in extreme poverty would impact a college student's spending decisions. While not everyone would have jumped to the same conclusion this administrator did, most would have been similarly befuddled. What my sophomore self had shared in the meeting was a point of view and a basis for decision-making that was so out of line with typical thinking on financial and life decisions that it didn't compute.

But why? The line of reasoning I had in mind, and that I shared with the director, has been around for millennia. It occupies space in the truisms of major world religions and in the common-sense understanding of everyday people. It's a concept that on the surface is so trite it feels almost silly to write about: we should help those less fortunate than us. We shouldn't waste while others want. Duh. From Ben Franklin to Buddha, from Jesus to Janis Joplin, it's been said countless times in countless contexts.

Why then was this director so nonplussed by my explanation that the best mental box she could categorize me into was "potential suicide case"? And why would most people give an equally quizzical look at anyone (at least any adult, as college students are expected to sometimes act in atypical ways) making a similar trade-off for a similar reason?

Probably because, like most truisms, the notion that we should give what we can to help those who are truly in need exists more in concept and story than in the actual decision-making of real people. It's the sort of idea that fits comfortably on an inspirational poster but sticks out like a sore thumb in day to day life. But again: why?

Jerusalem, circa 30 CE

What responsibility do we have to use our resources to help those who are suffering? And how do we think about that responsibility in light of the fact that there is an essentially limitless amount of suffering in the world?

Both religion and philosophy have taken a crack at answering those questions over the years. And within religion (we'll touch on philosophy later), there is perhaps no better starting point than Christianity. I am not Christian myself, and we will touch on Islam, Buddhism and other religious traditions shortly, but there are a few reasons to focus first and foremost on Christianity.

Christianity is still the world's largest religion by a significant margin, with 2.4 billion adherents. More importantly for our discussion, it is the most common religious belief among the world's richest 20 percent—a group which includes nearly all people in the English-speaking world and Western Europe, even those whose income falls below the poverty line in their respective countries. (This remains the case even after accounting for the fact that a dollar buys a lot less in a country like England than it does in a country like Sudan.)

Christianity is a great starting point for a second reason as well. While most major religions have passages that speak to the topic at hand, perhaps none have such clear and explicit answers to those questions attributed directly to God himself (in the form of Jesus Christ) as does Christianity.

Consider the following story from the Gospel of Luke, which is also recounted with nearly identical wording in the Gospel of Matthew:

> *Now a certain ruler asked Him, saying, "Good Teacher, what shall I do to inherit eternal life?"*
>
> *So Jesus said to him, "Why do you call Me good? No one is good but One, that is, God. You know the commandments: 'Do not commit adultery,' 'Do not murder,' 'Do not steal,' 'Do not bear false witness,' 'Honor your father and your mother.'"*
>
> *And he said, "All these things I have kept from my youth."*

So when Jesus heard these things, He said to him, "You still lack one thing. Sell all that you have and distribute to the poor, and you will have treasure in heaven; and come, follow Me."

But when he heard this, he became very sorrowful, for he was very rich.

And when Jesus saw that he became very sorrowful, He said, "How hard it is for those who have riches to enter the kingdom of God! For it is easier for a camel to go through the eye of a needle than for a rich man to enter the kingdom of God." (Luke 18:18–25 NKJV)

Here we have, for those who are Christian, a direct quote from God himself that could not be clearer on what those with resources to share should do: sell all that you have and distribute it to the poor.

Similar statements from Jesus on the matter can be found elsewhere in the Bible. Citing again from the Gospel of Luke:

"And the people asked him, saying, 'What shall we do then?' He answereth and saith unto them, 'He that hath two coats, let him impart to him that hath none; and he that hath meat, let him do likewise.'" (3:10–11 KJV)

Or consider the following quote attributed to Jesus in the Gospel of Matthew:

"When the Son of Man comes in his glory, and all the angels with him, he will sit on his throne in heavenly glory. All the nations will be gathered

before him, and he will separate the people one from another as a shepherd separates the sheep from the goats. He will put the sheep on his right and the goats on his left.

Then the King will say to those on his right, 'Come, you who are blessed by my Father; take your inheritance, the kingdom prepared for you since the creation of the world. For I was hungry and you gave me something to eat, I was thirsty and you gave me something to drink, I was a stranger and you invited me in, I needed clothes and you clothed me, I was sick and you looked after me, I was in prison and you came to visit me.'

Then the righteous will answer him, 'Lord, when did we see you hungry and feed you, or thirsty and give you something to drink? When did we see you a stranger and invite you in, or needing clothes and clothe you? When did we see you sick or in prison and go to visit you?'

The King will reply, 'I tell you the truth, whatever you did for one of the least of these brothers of mine, you did for me." (25:31–40 KJV)

As mentioned, I am not Christian myself (or religious in general), but I was raised Catholic and attended Catholic schools through high school. During those years, I occasionally heard these Bible passages—particularly the first, on how hard it is for a rich man to enter heaven—explained away as being more metaphorical than literal, a commentary on spiritual life rather than a directive for the specific action of giving what one has to the poor. That didn't seem like an honest view to me then, and it doesn't seem like an honest view to me now. The directive to give any extra one has to those who have less is highly specific. It is repeated multiple times in multiple settings, and the context of those settings supports a straightforward interpretation. Further, Jesus' apostles followed the advice literally, giving away what they had to the poor to then follow him.

Trying to explain away these statements from the biblical Jesus as conveying something other than their straightforward meaning always seemed to me to be clear-cut rationalizing by people who simply did not want to follow the directive. Such rationalizing even calls to mind the penultimate paragraph of the parable of the rich man: "But when he heard this, he became very sorrowful, for he was very rich." (Luke 18:23 NKJV)

For those who are Christian then—which is one out of every three human beings, two out of every three Americans, and the majority of the world's upper class—the idea that we should give all we can to help those who are suffering should be a very familiar concept. Given the extent to which Christianity has influenced Western Civilization, this concept should be familiar even to non-Christian westerners.

And yet, it is not. This way of thinking and living is so unfamiliar that it comes across as alien when carried out in real life, occasionally eliciting admiration but more often scoffing and incredulity. Why?

Two Premises

Before we go any further, it's worth highlighting two key premises that underlie this book.

In 1846, Danish philosopher Soren Kierkegaard penned the short but powerful treatise on devotion to Christianity, *Purity of Heart Is to Will One Thing*. In it, Kierkegaard argues the following: if you are truly Christian, and truly believe what that faith entails, then the only thing you should want is for God's will to be done. Your external actions and your internal mental life should therefore be focused on and striving toward that singular goal.

While Kierkegaard's book was a call-to-action on religious consistency, its general philosophical argument cuts deeper and has just as much value for those of no religious persuasion. At its core, Kierkegaard's invocation is a call to live a life consistent with one's beliefs. His point in a nutshell: if you believe something is both true and important, you should think through the logical conclusions of that belief and then live your life and base your desires and actions on those conclusions.

It's a straightforward concept, one that few would argue with, and one that almost no one lives by. When it comes to actually living it out, human psychology gets in the way. From mental heuristics that lead to errors in reasoning and judgment, to social influence, to biases in attention, to our innate drives to seek out comfort and status, the path from holding a strong existential, ethical, or religious belief to living a life that embodies the logical conclusions of that belief is an endless obstacle course. Sometimes the obstacles are imposed by the external world. But mostly they are internal, products of a brain that evolved hard-wired to help its owner survive a stone-age existence and before that a simian existence, not to help its owner live a life consistent with core beliefs.

While the two don't get lumped into the same bucket by modern philosophers or historians, Kierkegaard's argument dovetails well with another way of thinking about society and individual choices that began to circulate a century earlier: utilitarianism. This school of thought, articulated by philosophers John Stuart Mill and John Locke, argues that we as a society and we as individuals should strive to do the greatest good for the greatest number of people. The central question of a utilitarian approach to ethics is: How can we reduce the most hardship and increase the most well-being in the world around us?

Working forward from the core belief that we should strive to do the greatest good for the greatest number, Mill and Locke came to some conclusions that were significantly outside mainstream opinion in their day. Most prominently, they concluded that slavery and other discrimination based on race was wrong, that women should have equivalent rights to men, and that animals should be protected from abuse. For Mill and Locke (and of course many colleagues of theirs who did not happen to write well-known books), it was clear that if one wanted to do the greatest good for the greatest number then slavery, racism, sex discrimination and animal abuse needed to go. The fact that each of these bad practices was at the time well-enshrined in and staunchly defended by political law, religious teaching, and common practice made no difference.

The central challenge of any approach to ethics, including a utilitarian one, is taking our core belief to its logical conclusions, accepting those conclusions, and then living in line with and advocating for those conclusions. Doing so requires real discipline and mental work, a continual reassessing and resquaring of views and life choices with core beliefs. In the case of utilitarianism, it requires that we accept a constant grating against the accepted norms and conventional thought patterns of society, as well as a constant grating against our own human proclivities and wants. Successfully living out one's core beliefs—including a belief that we should do what we can to reduce the suffering of others—requires what Kierkegaard called "purity of heart" but might be more practically described as significant mental effort and self-discipline put in the long-term service of that key belief.

We've gone down this short philosophical path because the ideas espoused by Kierkegaard, Mill, and Locke underlie the two key premises of this book.

The first premise is that we should view something as good or bad based on the impact it has on others. The outcome of one's action is what matters most of all. Does the amount of suffering in the world decrease? Does the amount of well-being increase? If yes, the choice is probably ethically good. On the other hand, choices that lead to more suffering are probably ethically bad.

As with anything in the real world there are grey areas, situations where goods and harms are difficult to tease out or where goods and harms compete with one another. Different opinions on how good or bad a particular outcome is will lead to different conclusions on what is ethical and what isn't. But this approach at least gives a reasonable starting point to work from when deliberating between right and wrong.

Not everyone would agree with that premise. One person who would not agree is 18th century German philosopher Immanuel Kant, who is known as the father of the "categorical imperative." In Kant's view, the way to have a rational ethical system is to identify certain rules that are always true regardless of circumstance and then strictly adhere to those rules. In his own words, "Act only according to that maxim by which you can at the same time will that it should become a universal law."

Once the specific list of dos and don'ts has been established, the consequences one's actions have for others, and the context of a particular situation, do not need to be considered.

For example, Kant argued that it is wrong to lie and therefore one should never lie regardless of the circumstances. In an often-cited example of taking Kant's belief to its logical conclusion, if you're the family hiding Anne Frank in your attic and Nazi troops have knocked on your door, casually asking if you've seen any Jewish people being hidden in the neighborhood, you should tell the truth and admit that Anne is in your attic. Such an admission would result in her as well as you and your family (since you harbored her) being shipped off to a concentration camp. But since lying is universally wrong, the right thing to do in this situation is to tell the truth regardless of those consequences.

It's important to note that Kant's view was not that such an approach of "never lie" was good because on balance it led to the best overall outcomes in the world, despite the occasional bad results. His view was that there are certain actions that are inherently and universally good or bad. To live ethically is to follow the resultant dos and don'ts.

Moral guidelines laid down by major religions can be and sometimes are interpreted in a similar way, with a focus on specific dos and don'ts rather than on creating the best outcome. In theory (not necessarily in practice), morality in theistic religions is ultimately about carrying out the edicts of a deity, either through following the regulations established by that deity or by working to create the outcomes that deity desires. Sometimes, those directives are humanistic and track well with a goal of reducing suffering, such as directives to not kill or steal, or to care for the sick. At other times, the directives increase misery, with extreme examples including explicit instructions by deities to launch destructive wars, persecute those with same-sex attraction, and murder those who commit adultery or worship other deities. Many other directives focus on things that don't have much of an immediate positive or negative impact, such as requirements to believe in the deity or to attend religious services.

As noted, the ethical premise of this book is different from Kant's universal ethics from moralities grounded in religious doctrine. The first key premise is that something is good or bad based on the outcome it has on the world. Things that decrease suffering and increase well-being are generally good, and things that increase suffering are generally bad.

The second is that logical consistency is generally a good thing. In other words, Kierkegaard's advice is sound. If there is something that we believe is both true and important, we should think through the logical conclusions of that belief and try to live our lives based on those conclusions. We might consider this an existential premise. It is not going so far as to say like Socrates that "the unexamined life is not worth living." Rather, it is the premise that logical consistency is generally a good thing, including when it comes to ethics. We should strive toward consistency between our core beliefs and our daily actions, both because it's a more intentional and meaningful way to live and, more importantly, because it likely leads to better outcomes in the world.

This second premise also includes an assumption about you the reader. Some writers of books like this one will present a watered-down version of their ideas in order to be more palatable to and accepted by the majority of readers. Toward that end, they will pepper their pages with caveats and passages meant to prevent negative feelings or strong disagreement. An author might choose this approach to minimize defensiveness so that readers are more likely to absorb and consider the book's content; they may choose it out of a more general fear of offending others or causing discomfort; or they may choose it from a purely commercial desire to sell as many books as possible.

These approaches are understandable, but this book is not written in such a style. Instead, my assumption is that you have a healthy level of self-esteem and are not reading this book to feel good about yourself or to judge whether or not you are a "good" person. You're reading this book because you want to live a life in line with your own ethical beliefs, and you're open to being challenged with an idea on how to better do so. It assumes you prefer directness (done politely) over coddling, and hearing an earnest idea expressed frankly and fully—whether or not you agree with it—over a watered-down version which disrespectfully assumes you aren't capable of hearing anything stronger or aren't capable of making significant changes to your beliefs or lifestyle.

In summary, in writing this book I have assumed that you too want to live a life consistent with your ethics, that you want to do more good in the world, and that you view a new idea on how to do so as an opportunity and not as a threat. If that is indeed your reason for reading this book, thank you; I hope you find what you're looking for on the following pages.

CHAPTER TWO

The Fourth Box

*"Throughout history it has been
the inaction of those who could
have acted...that has made it
possible for evil to triumph."*
—HAILE SELASSIE

The Four Boxes

In thinking about the wealthy baron John Pierre and the ethics of the life he led, it can be helpful to picture a grid with four boxes. One axis of the grid can be labelled "Bad Things" and "Good Things". The second axis can be labelled "We Do" and "We Don't Do". We might view each of his ethically-meaningful life choices as falling into one of those four boxes.

In the first box we have Bad Things We Do. Occasions that fall into this box would include the times he lied, snapped angrily at his family, cheated a customer or business partner, and so on. These are the things that are easy for all of us to view as ethically negative.

In the second box we have Good Things We Do. Occasions that fall into this box would include his donations to the poor, kindness toward his family, fair treatment of his workers, and so on. These are the things that are easy for all of us to view as ethically positive.

In the third box we have Bad Things We Don't Do. These would be situations where John Pierre could have done something harmful—taken advantage of a customer, punched someone who insulted him, berated a family member who had wronged him—but refrained from doing so. While we don't think of these things much, they certainly matter—especially occasions where the bad thing that was not done would have been particularly harmful and where most people in John Pierre's shoes would have acted poorly.

Lastly, we have the fourth box: Good Things We Don't Do. These would be situations where John Pierre could have done good but failed to act. His failure to help fellow villagers who were starving—more explicitly his failure to share the resources he had with them, which resulted in prolonged suffering and death for many of them—would, of course, fall in this fourth box.

In reflecting on John Pierre's life and the glowing portrait painted of him at his funeral, something probably felt off to you. We can readily acknowledge and applaud the good things he did, as well as the fact that he refrained from doing harmful things to others. But we cannot ignore his failure to help those he had the ability to help, or the severe consequences of his inaction. What was conspicuously absent from the funeral speeches about John Pierre was a consideration of the fourth box.

Evaluating Ourselves

How would we think about ourselves and our own choices using the same four-box framework?

Evaluating ourselves in the first box, Bad Things We Do, is fairly easy. What things have we done that harmed others? All of us think at times about bad things we are doing or have done and typically feel regret for them. Improvement in this area is straightforward and something most of us strive for. We try to do fewer bad things, especially the particularly harmful ones. Bad things that we or others do are often plainly visible, have clear direct consequences, and in some cases violate explicit rules, laws, or doctrines. As a result, most moral attention—and nearly all of the moral approbation levied from religious, cultural, media and legal corners—is directed at this box.

Evaluating ourselves in the second box, Good Things We Do, is also easy. How many things are we doing that help others? All of us think occasionally about good things we are doing or have done—and typically feel the warm glow of satisfaction from having done them. Improvement in this area is also straightforward and something most of us think about on occasion. We try to at least periodically do good things for others. Most moral praise is directed at this box, at people who have done something viewed as ethically good. Much like the Bad Things We Do, the Good Things We Do are often plainly visible and sometimes have clear direct consequences.

The third box, Bad Things We Don't Do, is something you may not have thought much about. Moral approbation is obviously not directed at this box, but moral praise is rarely directed at it either. Because it's about refraining from action, there is often no action to view. And while we can more or less understand the consequences, those consequences are not as apparent or salient as those that result when we actively do something good or bad.

For some people, Bad Things We Don't Do is a locus of ethical attention and an area that contributes significantly to personal identity. Think, for example, of those who daily refrain from buying bottled water (to avoid causing pollution), driving (to avoid generating carbon emissions), buying products made overseas (to avoid the loss of American jobs), eating animal products (to avoid causing harm to animals), buying coffee that is not fair trade certified (to avoid the exploitation of workers), having sex before marriage (to avoid perceived impurity and violation of religious rules) and so on. Staying true to personal ethical commitments on avoiding causing harms—whether real or perceived—requires persistence and sacrifice. Many who do so incorporate that dedication into their self-identities. They view themselves as environmentalists, vegans, patriots, chastity movement participants (if there's a concise identity term for that, I'm not sure what it is), labor advocates and so on.

We can certainly give ourselves a pat on the back for areas where we are already actively and intentionally avoiding caus-ing real harms, and we can re-commit to staying the course. But such reflections at best maintain the status quo. When it comes to evaluating how we might live a *better* life, one more in line with our ethical values, the third box is simply not practically helpful. Mulling over the list of harmful things we could be doing but aren't fails to provide much actionable insight on changes we can make to do better.

The fourth box, Good Things We Don't Do, is something we have probably only thought about very occasionally. We might have turned down a request for a donation from a charity whose work we like, not made time to visit an elderly relative, or forgotten to phone a friend who was going through a difficult period and felt a small pang of remorse for our inaction. But few of us have thought very thoroughly or frequently about the fourth box.

What are the good things that we could be doing but are not? From a self-critical perspective, this is the question we must ask ourselves if we want to avoid the type of serious moral failure for which we condemned John Pierre. From an opportunistic perspective, asking ourselves this question, and answering it first with ideas and then with actions, unlocks opportunities for doing dramatically more good than we are doing now.

While this was not the case for 99 percent of human history, and still is not true for some people alive today, for those of us currently living in industrialized and semi-industrialized countries, the fourth box contains both our biggest ethical failings and our biggest opportunities for good. For each one of us, the suffering that is happening because of our failures to act is almost certainly worse than the suffering that happened because of any bad things we did directly. And the opportunity to do good that sits waiting in that fourth box is likely exponentially greater than the sum of any good things we've done thus far.

The reality is that when it comes to how we use our wealth and resources in the face of serious, preventable suffering, you are John Pierre and so am I.

Half a Billion Barons

For nearly everyone reading this, there is little difference between the ability John Pierre had to use his resources to prevent the suffering of others around him and our own ability to do the same today. You may not think of yourself as wealthy, but that's simply the result of narrowed perspective. Our psychological predilection is to pay attention to what's close to us, and chances are you're not dramatically wealthier than those you see around you day to day. But if we compare our wealth to that of many other people in the world, in particular the billion or so living in extreme poverty, the gap is just as wide as it was for John Pierre.

As noted earlier, over one billion people live on less than $2.50 per day, which adds up to $913 per year (including 280 million who live on less than $1.25 per day or $460 per year). Even someone working at the median minimum wage in the United States (roughly eleven dollars per hour, as most states have set state minimum wages that are higher than the federal minimum) earns twenty-five times more than that each year. The median US household income ($79,900 as of 2021) is almost ninety times higher, and most white-collar workers earn anywhere from one hundred to several hundred times more each year than one billion of their fellow global citizens.

Like John Pierre, we also live in a time with significant suffering, including starvation and poverty-related preventable death. And as was the case with John Pierre, we have the ability to use our resources to prevent a meaningful amount of that suffering from happening. Intervening to prevent some of the worst misery is just as easy for us as it would have been for him. There are effective charities, businesses, and other efforts that provide food, medicine, and (in some cases) direct cash transfers to people in the most dire need.

I've focused on extreme poverty and starvation because these are straightforward examples of suffering and they mesh easily with the John Pierre anecdote. But there are countless additional areas where our resources, if effectively used, can prevent or resolve other types of misery. In the human realm, this includes preventing or reversing blindness, debilitating disease, severe mental health issues, isolation in the elderly, and more. Other animal species also experience pleasure and pain, and there are cost-effective ways of reducing or preventing the suffering endured by large numbers of individual animals in factory farms and other industrial settings.

A family subsisting on two dollars a day in the mountains of Myanmar may not be knocking on our doors in the way peasants were at John Pierre's house. A mother pig immobilized for years in a crate where she is unable to turn around does not even have the ability to speak to us. But the geographic distances and the cultural and species differences that separate us from them does not alter the fact that they are there, they are suffering, and we have the ability to prevent that suffering— just as John Pierre had the ability to prevent the suffering of his fellow villagers.

John Pierre could have saved the lives and reduced the misery of dozens to perhaps hundreds of people. Those making even a median salary in the US, Western Europe, Korea, Japan, Australia, Malaysia, Singapore, and numerous other countries have the financial ability to do exactly the same. And those who would focus on preventing the suffering of animals, in particular farm animals, have the ability to benefit hundreds of thousands.

For a book-length discussion on our ability to save the lives of many other people through identifying and supporting cost-effective charities, see *The Life You Can Save* by the utilitarian philosopher Peter Singer. For general book-length discussions on a most-bang-for-your-buck approach to charity work and philanthropy, see *Doing Good Better* by Centre for Effective

Altruism co-founder William MacAskill or my previous book *How to Be Great at Doing Good*. As each book analyzes in its own way, it is by taking a rigorously calculated approach to giving that we can have an outsized impact. A handful of charities generate exponentially higher returns on investment than others—saving more lives, reducing more suffering, and adding more well-being for each dollar donated. These differences are not modest; particularly efficient charities can generate over ten thousand times more impact per dollar donated than less efficient ones.

Today, there are perhaps a half billion John Pierres around the world: people like you and me who have dramatically more wealth and resources than we need to survive in moderate comfort and happiness and who are surrounded by a large number of individuals who are suffering greatly due either to a lack of resources or to other problems we can help solve.

Meanwhile, if there was a dire need for help in John Pierre's time, the need today is even greater. There are many, many more individuals suffering today than in centuries and millennia past. That's not because things are getting worse (at least not for Homo sapiens). Things have been getting continually better across many measures of human health and welfare over the past decades and centuries, not just in the wealthiest countries but in the poorest countries as well. (For a hope-inducing book-length read on that, see Steven Pinker's *Enlightenment Now*.) Rather, there are many more individuals suffering today than in years past because of the continually increasing size of the human population, and because of that population's increasing industrialized use of animals.

The number of people living in extreme poverty today— defined as those living on under $1.90 per day—is larger than the total number of human beings that were alive on Earth just three hundred years ago. The number of people that will suffer to death from starvation and malnutrition or starvation-related diseases this year is larger than the total number of human beings that were alive on Earth ten thousand years ago. And when it comes to non-human animals, the number of individuals experiencing severe lifelong suffering in particularly cruel institutional settings (mainly factory farms) has increased at least a thousand-fold in the past century, going from near zero a few centuries ago to roughly 100 billion individuals today. So, while things are getting better in many ways for the average person, there is far more total human suffering in the world today and dramatically more animal suffering.

At the same time, as we will discuss momentarily, those of us in industrialized countries now have vastly more power to prevent or relieve suffering than at any other time in history. It is this combination of both increased suffering around us and greatly increased individual ability to prevent such suffering that makes the fourth box, Good Things We Don't Do, the area of both our greatest ethical failings and our greatest opportunities for good.

How You Became So Very, Very Powerful

The fourth box has not always been an area with such significant ethical consequences.

Looking particularly far back in the evolutionary chain, a toad living 300 million years ago was not really in a position—even if it had a brain suitable to have a flash of ethical inspiration—to make lives dramatically better for other toads. Similarly, chimps, bonobos, early hominids, and Homo sapiens for nearly the entirety of their existence had a pretty shallow fourth box to operate in. There was simply not much good they could do.

For most of human history, people lived in small groups and resources were sparse and fairly evenly distributed. A particularly altruistic hunter-gatherer in a tribe of one hundred forty members could go out of their way to provide additional comfort and kindness to sick members of the tribe, gather extra firewood, and so forth, but that was about it. With no additional resources to share, and such a tiny number of others around them, there was simply not much more good they could do. On the flip side, an apathetic member of the tribe could shirk communal duties by not sharing meat with others or not helping defend the tribe during an attack (and such shirking would probably be policed and punished by the group in the same way we might punish scofflaws today), but there was no significantly larger good that a tribe member could fail to carry out.

As agriculture-based civilizations and city-states grew over the past few millennia, wealth disparities sprang into existence, but with only a tiny percentage of the population falling into the wealthy category. Populations grew, and with that came the ability to interact with and impact more people, but the average person's reach was still largely confined to those in very close geographic proximity. A handful of new technologies emerged and better recording of information began, but neither was powerful or robust enough to have significant value for chipping away at serious social problems.

Compared to a hunter-gatherer living twenty thousand years ago, a typical citizen of ancient Rome would have had more people around them to potentially help (or fail to help). But the numbers were still relatively small. And given the average person's minimal financial resources at the time—a typical Roman citizen probably had little extra wealth to share beyond what they required for their own basic needs—they would not have had much to offer other than their time and limited knowledge. Further, when it came to sharing their time and knowledge, those resources could only go so far. Communication was limited to word of mouth and the occasional handwritten scroll (for the few that were literate), so influence and reach was largely limited to one's own city and surrounding villages. Knowledge was similarly limited. Our present-day understanding of the most basic factors affecting health and hygiene was completely unknown to those living just a few hundred years ago, let alone a few thousand.

For the vast majority of human history, there was little difference in wealth; humans were able to interact with and impact only a tiny handful of people; and there were no powerful communication technologies or institutional learning to leverage. Other than rare exceptions, such as kings, people simply did not have the ability to do great good for, or allow great harm to befall, a large number of others. The power to reduce the suffering on that scale did not exist, and so the failure to do so did not exist either.

It is only in the past couple of centuries, and particularly the past one hundred years, that several new realities emerged which gave people like you and me a dramatically outsized ability to do good (or allow harm). These factors have, together, moved the fourth box from ethically irrelevant to ethically all-important. These key factors include:

1. Large Populations: Dramatically larger human populations and the breeding of massive numbers of industrially confined animals.

2. Large Wealth Disparities: Large populations of the relatively wealthy co-existing with large populations in extreme poverty or with other challenges that resources can solve.

3. Modern Communications: Electronic communication tools that allow us to learn about and communicate with very large numbers of people anywhere on the planet, on top of widespread literacy and ease of language translation.

4. Increased Knowledge: A continually increasing body of shared scientific and other knowledge that allows beneficial work to be carried out and replicated more efficiently.

Consider how different our situation is from John Pierre's as a result of these four emergent realities. First, there are simply far more individuals suffering today than there were in John Pierre's time a mere five centuries ago. And while John Pierre was one of just a handful of people in his era that had significant wealth to share, today there are at least half a billion people whose wealth outstrips those of the less fortunate to a similar order of magnitude as John Pierre's outstripped his neighbors. Further, while John Pierre was only able to know about, interact with, and help those who lived near to him, today we can learn about, communicate with, and help individuals nearly anywhere on the planet. Finally, even for those within John Pierre's reach, the ways in which he could help them were likely simplistic and short term: providing money or food to those who needed it, and perhaps encouraging other wealthy merchants to do the same. Today, we have access to much more collective knowledge on what interventions can best alleviate problems such as crop failure and starvation in the short term and reduce their likelihood of reoccurrence in the future.

Now, regular people like you and me have dramatically more power to affect the lives of others than nearly any human being that lived from the dawn of Homo sapiens 100,000 years ago up through those living in the late 1800s. Even as recently as one hundred years ago, not a single human being had the ability to spare hundreds of people from blindness or to spare hundreds of thousands of animals from a lifetime of suffering. Today you do.

Expanding the lens beyond just the human species makes the uniqueness of our power even more clear. You have more power to produce happiness and reduce suffering in others than any of the untold quadrillions of non-human animals that have ever existed in the history of this planet. Birds are not in a position to help heal another bird that gets a broken wing, let alone help end starvation among humans or provide food to a starving deer. As intelligent as they are, pigs cannot help themselves or other pigs escape the suffering of life on a factory farm, let alone reduce human poverty in various parts of the world. You, on the other hand, can ease the suffering of hundreds if not many hundreds of thousands of others, human and non-human animal alike. Are you feeling powerful yet?

You should be. You and I now have the power to do an incredible amount of good, an amount unthinkable to people of even a few decades past. And that is exactly why the fourth box has become so ethically consequential. As Peter Parker (aka *Spider Man*'s) Uncle Ben famously stated in that comic book franchise, "With great power comes great responsibility."

When we fail to act, when we leave that power unused and that good undone, when we let harm and suffering befall others even though we have the ability to prevent it, we are making the same choice that John Pierre did in turning the starving farmers away from his door. Failing to use our power, declining to use the great resources at our disposal to address the incredible suffering just outside our door, is just as much of an ethical failure for us as it was for John Pierre. And as was the case for John Pierre, our inactions have far more serious consequences for those around us than any good or bad actions that we do directly.

Yes, the good things we are doing now matter. The good things we do for our family, friends, colleagues, and the people we interact with over the course of a year, the donations we make, the hours we spend volunteering—all of these things matter. We should keep doing these.

And yes, the bad things we do certainly matter as well. The emotional or physical harm we may cause to others, the negative direct and indirect impacts our choices can have on other people, on non-human animals, and on the environment— these things are important as well. We should work harder to minimize the harm we cause.

But the good we are doing now pales in the comparison to the good we could be doing but are not: saving numerous lives, giving dozens of people back the gift of sight, freeing hundreds of thousands of animals from a lifetime of abusive conditions. And the harms we are causing directly to others with our bad actions pale in comparison to the harms others continually endure as a result of our inactions.

If we want to do more good in the world we should focus our attention on the fourth box, on the good things we could do but are not yet doing. If we want to reduce suffering in the world, we should focus our attention on the fourth box: the suffering that is happening right now because of our daily decisions to turn away and refrain from sharing our resources.

Our actions have consequences. Our inactions have even greater ones.

CHAPTER THREE

The Roots of
Our Inaction

*"The apathy of the people is
enough to make every statue leap
from its pedestal, and to hasten
the resurrection of the dead."*
—WILLIAM LLOYD GARRISON

Evolutionary Psychology

Aside from a few basic obligations, like caring for one's children and paying taxes, there are no legal obligations to share one's resources with others. And other than providing for one's family, there are nearly no social expectations when it comes sharing one's resources either. Why? Why do we as individuals and we as societies pay so little attention to the fourth box, given how consequential it is for those around us? And why do we share so relatively little of our resources with those who are suffering in the first place? The most fundamental answer to both questions can be found in evolutionary psychology.

Evolutionary psychology is a field within the social sciences that works from the principle that just as our physical bodies have been molded by the forces of evolution, selecting for the traits that best enabled individual and genetic kin group survival, so too have our minds. We have the thoughts, feelings, mental processes, and mental biases we do because evolution selected for them. They were ways of feeling, thinking, and processing that made our ancestors more likely to survive and reproduce. Environment, culture, and individual genetic variation play large shaping roles as well. But if we want to understand why people think and act the way they do, it's important to consider the evolutionary forces that may have shaped those preferences and proclivities.

When looking at the influence of evolution on present-day behavior, those in the evolutionary psychology field use two different lenses to view the same phenomenon. The first lens looks at the evolutionary reasons why our minds would have evolved a particular tendency or drive. This is termed the *root cause*. The second lens looks at how that tendency or drive feels and functions at the surface level in our day to day life. This is termed the *proximate cause*.

For a prototypical example of root cause versus proximate cause, we can look at sexual desire and sexual pleasure. From an evolutionary perspective, our mammalian ancestors who derived some feeling of pleasure from the act of reproducing, and who therefore had more desire to engage in it (i.e. sexual desire), likely mated more often. This led them to have more children and pass on more genetic copies of themselves than did individuals who experienced minimal or no sexual desire.

Over a long period of time, this led to increased sexual desire throughout the population. In evolutionary psychology terms, this is the root cause of sexual desire. It was evolutionarily advantageous to our distant ancestors because it increased mating and reproduction.

In our day-to-day life though, we're not typically pursuing sex because we view it as an effective strategy for passing on our genes. We crave sex because it's pleasurable on several levels. In evolutionary psychology terms, this is the proximate cause of sexual desire.

Many of our psychological predispositions—from the types of work and play that interest us, to the types of faces and bodies we find attractive, to the situations that make us feel agitated—can be traced back in part to evolutionary root causes. These root causes manifest today in proximate causes, the mental drivers that steer us toward one thing and away from another.

Evolutionary psychology can help shed light on why we pay such little attention to the fourth box and to harms of inaction. As a basic starting point, we can see the clear evolutionary roots of why those of us with extra resources don't feel naturally included to share them with anyone other than our families and close friends. We don't want to take from what we have and give to the poor for the same reason Happy Meals come with a side of French fries and not a side of broccoli. Just as our evolutionary heritage has hardwired us to crave foods high in fat, salt, and sugar since gorging on such foods when they were available helped our distant ancestors survive, so too our evolutionary heritage has hardwired us to horde resources for ourselves and our family and to be stingy with strangers.

Pro-social species, including humans, emerged specifically because of the survival benefits that came from members of a small group working cooperatively together. If I give someone in my small tribe a piece of meat or a nice arrowhead for a spear, they are more likely to do the same for me in the future. In a pre-agricultural world, this social insurance policy was incredibly important. For much of human history, helping those in close proximity was not just beneficial but often necessary for survival. As a result, not only was sharing of resources and responsibilities among tribe members encouraged, it was required, with shirkers being ostracized and if need be expelled from the tribe. Over time, the selection pressure this applied formed part of the evolutionary root cause for our drive to help those who are near to us, primarily family and close friends.

Conversely, helping those in another tribe—for example a group of hunter-gatherers who lived thirty miles to the north— did far less to boost our ancestors' chances of survival. Doing so could even have been counterproductive at times, as those in other tribes were (at the least) competitors for resources and (at worst) enemies that could physically attack. It's not surprising then that evolution baked into our minds relatively little concern for strangers. Favors directed at those who would surely never be able to reciprocate and who clearly did not share many of the same genes—such as individuals living far away, and individuals of any other species—simply had no genetic payoff throughout human history.

As a result, a strong drive to help family and kin and a strong disinclination to share resources with strangers now comes standard in the human genetic makeup. Many of us would feel guilty if we forgot to give our mother a Mother's Day card but feel nothing if we failed to send money to help a child facing starvation in another country. Today nearly all of our income and resources are used for the benefit of ourselves and our family, with only a trivial amount shared with others, even when our families are well-off and those others are in desperate need. In the United States, one of the world's wealthiest nations per capita and also one with an above-average rate of charitable giving, contributions average just three percent of annual income. That percentage has barely budged over the past seventy years, despite the very large increase in inflation-adjusted per capita wealth in the same period. Other than taxes, the remaining 97 percent of our incomes are spent first on basic necessities and then on providing comforts and pleasures to ourselves and our family. The fact that taxation itself would never work if it was voluntary, and instead must be a legal obligation punishable by jail time, is itself a telltale sign of just how loathe we are to share our resources. It is only when a state imposes strong punishments for not paying, and thereby creates a compelling self-interest to pay, that most people can be made to contribute to the public good in a significant fashion.

While these tendencies to help (or not help) others may have their root cause in survival and reproduction, the way they are felt day to day is quite different. When we buy a box of Girl Scout cookies from a neighborhood child selling them at our door or donate to our local United Way or food pantry, we are probably not doing so because we think it will increase our odds of survival. Instead, we are probably feeling some mixture of empathy, desire to help, guilt, social obligation, a desire to look good, or so on. These are the proximate causes of why we do good for and share our resources with others. (For a discussion on the problems of using empathy as a guide for charitable giving and ethics generally, see the book *Against Empathy* by Paul Bloom.)

On the other hand, when presented with opportunities to help those who are far removed from us geographically, culturally or otherwise, those feelings of empathy, social obligation, and so on are relatively muted. Given the lack of a strong evolutionary root cause, our drive to help strangers is weaker than our drive to help those near to us, which itself is dramatically weaker than our drive to prioritize ourselves and our family. And it shows. Of that 3 percent sliver of American incomes that is donated to help others, the majority is directed at local charitable efforts. A vanishingly small percentage of our resources—less than a third of charitable giving and well under 1 percent of total income—goes toward helping those who are suffering outside of one's own community.

This is particularly unfortunate today given those who have the resources to provide significant help and those who are most in need of help are often quite separated from one another. Countries with the highest per capita income are generally far removed geographically and, in many instances, also removed ethnically and culturally from countries with the lowest per capita income. There are certainly exceptions, countries such as India or Brazil that have a thriving upper middle and upper class living alongside and, at times, mere blocks away from large numbers of people in extreme poverty. But these are the exceptions. And even in these countries, economic, cultural, and family divides keep the wealthy and the poor largely separated socially, if not physically.

As wide as the gulf may be between people in San Francisco and people in South Sudan, the gulf between humans and non-human animals is even more extreme. While animal suffering is not necessarily far removed geographically from people with the ability to end that suffering, it largely occurs out of sight. More importantly, the lack of genetic relatedness is obvious: non-human animals are not even part of our own species, let alone our community.

Humans care little about other species for the same root-cause reason they care little about people living far away. With rare exceptions, such as possibly the early domestication of wolves, throughout human history benevolence toward individuals of other species would have had no survival benefit and, therefore, no reason to become a part of human mental hard-wiring. As a result, few people feel the same level of empathy, distress, or social compunction to help animals as they do for other humans, even though there are not dramatic differences in the capacity for suffering between humans and many other animal species. The psychological bridge between humans who have the resources to help and non-human animals who endure intense suffering is a very long one.

Even though today there is no need to gorge on fat, salt, and sugar beyond a certain modest amount, and (conversely) doing so can actually cut our lives short, we retain an almost overwhelming compulsion to eat foods high in those three things. It takes significant willpower to restrain ourselves from doing so. Similarly, even though today for many of us there is no need to horde resources beyond a certain modest amount, and doing so results in many other people suffering needlessly, we retain an almost overwhelming compulsion to keep nearly all of the resources we acquire for ourselves and our family. It takes significant willpower to restrain ourselves from such needless hoarding.

The proximate cause, or how this all feels in day to day life, is readily known by all of us. We want to buy things, experiences, and environments that give us pleasure, security, comfort, higher social status, and the like, and to receive the attendant emotional benefits (sometimes real, sometimes imagined) that we think those things will bring. And we want to hold on to resources we don't need now so that we and our families can be assured we'll be able to continue buying those things we want far into the future. We crave and are drawn to those things and that use of resources in much the same way we crave and are drawn to French fries over broccoli. Giving our resources away to those we don't know seems far less enjoyable than using them for ourselves or our family. And it may well be less pleasant in some instances.

That said, we are also quite bad predictors of what will make us happy. While it's outside the scope of this book, I'd wager that for most people giving away dramatically more resources would initially feel less pleasant but, once adjusted to, would increase overall long-term happiness and well-being—much like choosing broccoli over French fries nine times out of ten.

Taking an evolutionary psychology perspective can help us understand why we are so reluctant to share our resources, even when we have so much. It can also help us understand why the fourth box, inaction even in the face of suffering, can register so dimly on our ethical radar. At the same time, as reasoning individuals, we can probably agree that evolution is not destiny.

Our intuitive sense of ethics, like our emotions and our operating intelligence, was crafted into its current shape because that shape had evolutionary advantages in years past. We can appreciate that and have some respect for the wisdom of ways of thinking that helped our species survive and thrive.

But we can also acknowledge that life today is in certain ways very different from what it was for early humans, pre-human primates, and the smaller mammals that preceded them. Things are very different today from what they were even a few hundred years ago, let alone a few thousand or a few million. We have dramatically more secure lives and a far, far greater amount of resources, both individually and collectively. We can use our reasoning to reconsider the best balance between using our resources to protect ourselves and our families and using them to help others who are suffering intensely. We can say "no thanks" to some of the drives and dispositions that helped our ancestors survive in millennia or even centuries past but that are no longer needed for our own survival today.

Evolution has left us with many mental predispositions that we as a civilization have been working hard to strip away or ignore. These include prejudice against people of races other than our own, dislike and distrust of those who are less physically attractive, and an inclination to use violence to resolve conflicts and achieve dominance, to name just a few. The predisposition to hoard far more resources than we need, even when we know that many others will suffer intensely or die as a result of our failure to share, is a similar piece of evolutionary baggage that we would do well to reason our way out of or co-opt as best we can.

Ethics Fast and Slow

Some of the mental hardwiring that evolution has left us with is as straightforward as strong directives to "have sex," "eat fatty foods," and "keep resources for yourself." Other bits are more nuanced, and their impacts are more subtle. This latter category includes the ways our brains process information, make assumptions, and draw conclusions, processes that are in operation in all of the thought work we do—including when thinking about what's good and bad and when making ethically consequential decisions.

These mental processes are not perfectionist in nature. Instead, our brains tend to use simple heuristics, rules of thumb that allow for fast judgments while generally avoiding catastrophic mistakes. These processes are sometimes called cognitive biases because they operate just like any other bias. They work largely outside the realm of conscious awareness; they incline us strongly in a certain direction; and we can make serious errors in judgment if we don't vigilantly keep in mind that they are operating behind the scenes.

Our brains use these mental heuristics because they've been advantageous for survival. For one thing, they are an efficient way to make decisions. Given the overwhelming number of discrete decisions each of us has to make every day—whether to brush our teeth or shower first, whether we should buy a new toothbrush, which bar of soap to use, how long to wash our hair, how long to spend fixing up our hair, whether we should change our hair style, what to make for breakfast…and these are all before the day really even starts—if we took the time to carefully think through each decision, our lives would grind to a halt. Mental heuristics are an efficient tool for making mundane decisions when the personal stakes are low.

One of the most common mental heuristics used when making a decision is to simply repeat a similar decision we made before. If we run out of toothpaste and have to buy more, chances are we will buy the same brand we bought last time (unless we really disliked it). We won't re-examine all forty options in the toothpaste aisle every time we need more tooth-paste. The time cost of doing so wouldn't be worth the benefit.

Mental heuristics are also helpful for figuring out what to pay attention to. There is a huge amount of visual, auditory, tactile, and olfactory stimuli that surrounds us at all times. We are also bombarded with written and verbal information, which today streams toward us at record pace from billboards, television, the internet, radio stations, newspapers, books, and the mouths of those around us. It would be excruciatingly difficult, if not impossible, to continually put conscious consideration into whether to pay a lot, a little, or basically no attention to each individual informational input. Instead, our brains use rules of thumb to help make those decisions for us quickly and without much deliberative thought. If we hear a huge crash behind us, we turn around. Here, the unconscious mental heuristic we are using is to pay attention to noises that are loud and unexpected. On the flip side, if we sit in a coffee shop reading the morning paper, our brains will allow the dozen conversations happening around us to fade so fully from our conscious attention that we don't even hear them.

When we're making an important decision or facing a novel problem that's hard to make a snap judgment on, our brains shift away from heuristics and into more careful analytical consideration. This intentional reasoning takes longer and requires a lot more processing power, but it can get us to a more accurate understanding of the situation and a better decision. If we are buying a new home, we will almost certainly engage this careful analytical processing as we consider the pros and cons of any particular house (supplemented, as always, by a lot of mental heuristics along the way).

Researcher Daniel Kahneman has termed these two very different mental processing routes the *fast route* and the *slow route*. Over the past several decades, Kahneman and other researchers have conducted numerous studies to identify and understand the cognitive biases our brains rely on when engaging in fast-route mental processing. In his encyclopedic tome *Thinking, Fast and Slow*, Kahneman categorizes fifty-two such biases that seem to come standard in the human brain, reappearing across numerous cultures and contexts. While these biases seem to have developed because they are generally advantageous, there are many situations where they backfire and lead us to inaccurate judgments and bad decisions. By better understanding what these biases are and how and when they operate, we can better notice when we're being steered by one of them—and therefore when we may want to engage more careful analytical consideration to make sure we're not coming to faulty conclusions.

While this differs from the types of biases Kahneman explores, probably all of us have come across one well-known example of a nonconscious heuristic at work in the area of visual information processing. There are numerous versions of the same basic experiment, but the most common one involves a pair of lines situated above and below one another. Line A has arrows on each end, short lines that cut diagonally inward from each end of the line. Line B has reverse arrows on each end, short lines that stretch diagonally outward from each end of the line. In the experiment, viewers are asked to guess whether Line A or Line B is longer. To the eyes, Line B seems clearly to be longer than Line A.

The trick, of course, is that both lines are exactly the same length. It is the additional visual information around Line A and Line B, namely the inward or outward facing arrows at the ends of each line, that tricks the eyes into seeing Line B as longer. The heuristic at play here involves our visual processing system using broader context cues to make judgments about any specific piece of the visual puzzle. In most cases, this results in more accurate visual processing. Our distant ancestors whose visual processing systems evolved this approach were better able to understand and navigate their environments, leading to higher survival rates and the passing on of these nonconscious visual processing rules until they became standard in the gene pool.

But clearly in certain situations, such as the experiment above, that visual processing heuristic backfires. Being aware of that heuristic, and understanding why it works the way it does, is what allows us to watch out for it and prevent it from leading us to faulty conclusions. Participants who are given the experiment a second time are not fooled again. While Line B may still look longer initially, awareness of the bias leads to a closer inspection of the lines and the ultimate realization that they are actually the same length.

Just as our visual processing system evolved certain heuristics that worked well evolutionarily but sometimes lead to (surprisingly) incorrect visual conclusions, so too our more general mental processing system evolved heuristics that worked well evolutionarily but sometimes lead to faulty results. These are the cognitive biases in the realms of thought, feeling, judgment, and decision-making that Kahneman's work explores.

One example of a cognitive bias from Kahneman's list of fifty-two is the *endowment effect*. This bias leads us to value things that we already have much more highly than things we don't yet have. In one academic study designed to surface the endowment effect, a researcher showed a group of students a mug and asked them what price they would be willing to pay to buy the mug. Their answers averaged around $2.50. To them, the mug was worth $2.50. A separate group of students were all given the exact same mug for free by the researcher at the start of the session. The researcher than asked them to name the lowest price at which they would be willing to sell the mug back to him. The average answer: $5.25. To this group, the mug was worth $5.25.

If our brains were behaving purely logically, in the fashion of Homo economicus, the two prices should have been very close to one another. What is it about a mug that would make it double in perceived value from $2.50 to $5.25 the moment we own it? Since there is nothing about the mug itself that changes, what must be changing is our perception of the mug—a cognitive bias at work. Study after study has demonstrated this so-called endowment effect, our seemingly innate and nearly universal tendency to value a particular thing much more highly when we own it than when we don't. (I say nearly universal because in a few remote tribes, where personal possessions regularly cycle through to other members of the tribe, the endowment effect does not seem to exist. When what you have is constantly being taken away from you, it probably makes sense to stop getting attached to it.)

Like with any cognitive bias, we could speculate about why valuing something we have more highly than something we don't have could have delivered some evolutionary advantage for our distant ancestors. Perhaps it's a bias toward conservatism that made sense in a more precarious and resource-scarce world: I know the sack full of tubers I have in my hut are good, nutritious ones that will feed me for a week. Giving them to you means taking a major risk by giving up my storehouse of food. The tubers you want to give me may turn out to be good, but they may turn out to be mostly rotten.

This a somewhat flippant layman's example; the actual suspected causes and outcomes of the endowment effect are far more nuanced than this. But the general point is that the mental heuristics we developed as a species are sensible, and they generally lead to good decisions, at least in certain contexts. But context here is key. A mental bias that works well in one situation may fail terribly in another. A heuristic that was advantageous for hunter-gatherers twenty thousand years ago is not necessarily advantageous to those of us in wealthy industrialized civilizations today. In fact, such heuristics can be and often are harmful, leading us to make subpar decisions that waste our money, harm our health, and reduce our happiness— all without making us one bit more likely to pass on our genes or live longer.

The dozens of cognitive biases that come standard in the human brain aren't just at play when we're considering buying or selling a mug. They are also at play when we're reflecting on ethics and on whether we are living a good life. Consider, for example, another one of Kahneman's fifty-two biases: *attentional bias.*

There are numerous mental heuristics our brains use in determining what to pay attention to, and these typically operate outside the realm of conscious reflection. As noted earlier, we are much more likely to pay attention to things that are uncommon and dramatic than to things that are common and less dramatic. This is true not only of direct auditory cues (for example, a loud bang) but also of information generally. A terrorist attack that kills five people in California will dominate national headlines, whereas a car crash that kills five people in California will not even generate significant regional news coverage. Five people dying in California from preventable hypertension won't make the news at all. The identical real-world consequence of each incident—five people lost their lives—is not a key factor in which of these stories gets our attention. Rather it's the suddenness, violence, and rarity of each incident that makes it more or less interesting to readers and, therefore, to news editors.

The same bias carries through into public policy. Consider the amount of money spent by the US government in the twenty years following 2001 to reduce isolated acts of terrorism, which kill a couple hundred people per year on average (even after factoring in 9/11). The amount of funding that has gone toward preventing similar attacks dwarfs the amount of money spent by the government in the same period to reduce automotive deaths (which kill tens of thousands of people per year) or to prevent premature deaths caused by poor diet (which number in the hundreds of thousands per year). The proportionality of response to each of these threats is clearly not based on the severity of the consequences, at least not in terms of the number of people that died. So, what is that level of response based on? While of course there are many factors, one factor is how strongly each of these threats triggers our cognitive biases.

Our brains have been honed by evolution to pay attention to things that stick out from the typical background environment. When a lion poked its head out of a distant tree line, our ancestors needed to notice that quickly. Our brains have been honed to pay much more attention to sudden, fast-moving risks (consider again the lion, or an attacking member of another clan) than to long-term, slow-moving ones. We use social cues to assess threats as well, paying greater attention to the risks that others around us are talking about. These are just three examples of attention-related biases that evolution has carved into our cognitive processing systems because of the survival advantage they had earlier in our evolutionary history.

When we are thinking about what is good and bad, and how good or how bad a certain thing is, attentional biases come strongly into play. Bad actions that pull the strings of our attentional bias are more likely to get our attention and to generate stronger condemnation. Sudden, forceful, and uncommon short-term harms grab our attention and outrage in a way that commonplace and slow-moving harms do not, even if the latter ultimately cause far more damage.

Moreover, as noted just above, when a particular ethical area receives a lot of public attention, it can snowball into further-increased attention. This is an attention-related bias with its own term: *salience bias*. When it comes to ethics, salience bias can lead us to focus intently on the publicly prominent social issues of the day, to be acutely outraged by them, and to more strongly condemn perceived bad actions in those areas. We pay far less attention to, and are far less outraged by, issues that are not prominently in the public forum—even if those issues cause exponentially more harm.

Salience bias can also lead people to dramatically overestimate the frequency or scale of a particular problem. For example, a poll conducted by news site *Skeptic.com* found that in the wake of widespread media coverage of police killings of African Americans in 2020, approximately one-quarter of Americans believed one thousand or more unarmed African Americans were killed by police each year, and 10 percent believed ten thousand or more were killed each year. Among the very liberal, over half believed one thousand or more where killed each year, and close to a quarter believed ten thousand or more were killed each year. The actual number, according to the *Washington Post*, was twelve. Other polls have found similarly dramatic over-estimations of problems by both politically conservative and politically liberal groups when it came to hot-button issues that were receiving significant media coverage. This is not to imply that such killings, or similar avoidable killings and abuse, are not a serious problem. It's merely meant to point out the way salience bias can lead us to overestimate how frequent a particular type of occurrence may be.

Circling back to the focus of this book, attentional bias and salience bias probably also incline us to pay far more attention to actions than to inactions. Inactions are almost never going to pull the strings of our attention bias. There is nothing sudden, forceful, or out of the ordinary occurring since there is nothing occurring at all. Inaction and the consequences of that inaction are also usually far removed from one another in space and time, significantly diluting our brain's ability to register the connection, let alone view the inaction as ethically bad. And since we look to social cues to consider what harms to pay attention to, the fact that harms of inactions are rarely talked about and virtually never condemned creates a self-reinforcing cycle of non-concern. Attention to the severe consequences of inaction remains minimal at best.

Attentional bias and salience bias are not the only cognitive biases that lead us to ignore the ethics of inaction. Other biases likely at play include the following:

> *Affect Heuristic*: Our emotions in the moment can significantly influence our judgments and decisions, a bias referred to as the affect heuristic. As one consequence

of this, the more of a negative emotional charge we get from thinking about something, the more ethically problematic we are likely to think it is. Because the harms that result from inaction are usually very separated in time and place from the inaction, and because inaction is a yawningly normal state of affairs, we're unlikely to feel flashes of guilt, distress, or similar emotions when thinking about that inaction. That lack of emotional charge can contribute to a feeling that inaction is not problematic. It can also lead us to conclude that nothing particularly bad is really going to happen when we fail to act.

Bandwagon Effect and Social Norms: The well-known bandwagon effect bias refers to the phenomenon in which the more popular and widespread an opinion becomes, the more likely we are to adopt the same viewpoint. We also tend to follow the behavior of those in our community, a proclivity that has been termed the social norms bias. Given the near-universal current opinion is that we have no responsibility to share more than a token amount of our resources with others outside our family, we are strongly inclined to adopt that same majority viewpoint (if we even stop to consider this question in the first place). And given that most people in our communities use nearly all of their resources on themselves, we are likely to do the same.

Cognitive Dissonance: We like to think that our beliefs line up well with one another and with our actions into one coherent, sensible whole. When we come across an apparent mismatch between our beliefs and our behavior, generating an uncomfortable feeling termed cognitive dissonance, we try to find a way to resolve that discord. As changing our behavior usually seems difficult, we are biased toward rationalizing our way out of the conflict instead, persuading ourselves that there is no contradiction between our beliefs and behavior.

Since most people view themselves as ethically good, and most do not share a meaningful amount of their resources with others in need, there are just a few routes our minds can take to resolve the cognitive dissonance we may feel between that belief and that behavior. First, we can look for reasons to disregard or refute the argument that it's ethically important to share a more significant amount of our resources with those in need. If the argument is flawed, then there is no contradiction between our failure to share and our belief that we are good people. Second, we can look for reasons why the argument may be generally true but does not apply in this particular situation; for example, we may tell ourselves we plan to give more to others later in life when we are more financially well-off. Lastly, we could accept that the argument is true and then make the significant change in behavior for which the argument calls. But as significant behavior change is always difficult, the first two routes—both of which rationalize away the mismatch—are far more appealing and are the routes we are biased toward taking.

Identifiable Victim Effect: We are much more likely to help a specific individual in need than we are to help a group of individuals, a bias dubbed the identifiable

victim effect. Charities with a sophisticated fundraising program are aware of this bias, and it is the reason
so many charitable appeals focus on a specific child,
widow, family, refugee, dog, or so forth. Studies have
consistently shown that doing so significantly increases
donations.

Bad actions typically have clearly identifiable victims,
the individual or set of individuals who suffered the
consequences of the bad actions. On the other hand,
those who suffer as a result of inaction are often the
textbook definition of a vague group. There is a teem-
ing mass of humans and animals around the world
enduring utter misery, and inaction on our part is
impossible to connect to specific suffering endured by
specific individuals within that mass. Because there is
usually no clear identifiable victim of inaction, we are
biased toward viewing failures of inaction as ethically
non-problematic.

In-Group Bias: Earlier we discussed how evolutionary
psychology has molded our minds to have strong concern for our immediate family, modest concern for our
immediate community, and relatively little concern
for strangers. That psychological disposition is known
as the in-group bias, and its effects extend beyond
just how genetically related we are to others. We tend
to care much more about those who are part of our
"in-group"—those who are close to us personally, culturally, ethnically, politically, or geographically—than
those who are not close to us in those ways. Since most
individuals experiencing particularly acute suffering

are far removed from us on several of these dimensions (and a large subset of them are not even the same species as we are), the in-group bias can leave us less motivated to help them.

Central to our discussion is one final cognitive bias: the *omission bias*. The omission bias is the well-documented human characteristic of reacting more strongly to harmful actions than to harmful omissions. This includes judging acts of commission more harshly than acts of omission, even when the harms that result are the same. Sound familiar? What you are reading is essentially a book-length discussion of omission bias in ethics—its causes, its consequences, and its implications for the world and for ourselves.

Studies conducted on omission bias have been wide-ranging. One study looked at parents who decided not to vaccinate their children out of concern for the small risk of death that comes with vaccination. Even though their children's chances of dying were much higher if they did not get vaccinated than if they did get vaccinated (because the disease is a significantly greater threat than the vaccine), the study found that these parents refrained from vaccinating their children in part due to the omission bias. These parents were significantly more uncomfortable with the thought that their children might die as a result of their action (getting them vaccinated) than the thought that their children might die as a result of their inaction (not getting them vaccinated).

Another study on the omission bias found that NBA referees are 50 percent less likely to call fouls during the final minutes of professional basketball games. In those critical waning minutes, refs are more worried about tipping the final outcome of a game through action (calling a foul) than they are about tipping the final outcome through inaction (not calling a foul), even though calling or not calling a borderline foul has an equal potential impact on the game's outcome.

Studies on omission bias have also looked at ethical judgments on actions versus inactions. In one study, participants were asked to consider a hypothetical scenario where two tennis players are having a meal together shortly before facing off in a championship match. "Pete" knows that "Andre" has a bad food allergy that if triggered, would debilitate his performance in the upcoming match. Further, Pete notices that one of the dishes on the menu has the allergenic ingredient. Half of the study participants were told that Pete encouraged Andre to eat the dish, knowing that it would cause a reaction that hurt his performance on the court. The other half of the study participants were told that Pete saw Andre order the allergenic dish and chose not to say anything about it. Both sets of participants were asked to assess whether Pete did something ethically bad, and how bad it was.

The consequence of both scenarios was identical: Pete made a deliberate choice, the result of which was that Andre got sick. But participants in the first group (who were told Pete actively encouraged Andre to eat the dish) judged Pete much more critically than participants in the second group. Although the real-world consequence was identical, a bad action was judged to be far worse than a bad inaction. Similar studies have found the same pattern of ethical judgment when comparing harmful actions to equally harmful inactions.

The omission bias and the other cognitive biases that come into play when making ethical judgments and ethically consequential decisions help explain why we as individuals and we as societies generally fail to pay attention to the harms that result from inaction. Reflecting on these biases can also lead us to a much broader realization: our ethical judgments on what is good and what is bad, on how good and how bad those things are, on what is ethically important and what is ethically irrelevant, are in many cases wildly out of sync with real-world consequences like suffering endured or well-being experienced by others around us.

Most of us think that determinations of what's good, what's bad, and what's really bad are generally common sense. But our individual and collective "common sense" views on right and wrong are merely the evolutionary and cultural product of human brains. And those brains' judgments, feelings, and decisions are heavily guided by cognitive processes and mental heuristics that evolved into being because they helped small bands of apes and hominids survive in pre-historic savannahs. There was little evolutionary selection pressure toward having logically consistent views on ethics, or toward living in a way that best reduced suffering in the world.

Put more simply, ethical intuitions come from the human mind, and the human mind is not optimized for ethics. The human mind is optimized for surviving and passing on genes in a nomadic pre-agrarian environment.

Imagine that the world's best chess player, who emerged as the world's best after years of training and practice and repeatedly beating better and better players, was asked to write a blockbuster movie script. The results would probably not be very good. Sure, there are some mental skills from the chess world that could be helpful; but in general, the attributes and capabilities that make for a chess grand champion are quite different from the attributes and capabilities that make for an Oscar-winning screenwriter. A person trained and selected over time for chess-playing ability is unlikely to be a naturally excellent screenwriter. Similarly, Homo sapiens—trained and selected over time for survival on the savannah and not for ethical consistency or altruism—are not in their element when it comes to ethics.

This realization should cause us to view "common sense" ethical wisdom, and our intuitive sense of right and wrong, with caution. Many of our intuitions are likely to be out of sync—sometimes dramatically so—with real-world consequences of suffering and happiness. Many socially agreed-upon views on what's ethically important and ethically irrelevant are similarly out of sync. And that includes our views on the importance and ethical valence of actions versus the importance and ethical valence of inactions.

Religion and Law

Just as cognitive biases can cause our individual sense of right and wrong (and of what matters ethically and what doesn't) to be out of sync with real-world consequences, they can also lead religious decrees, judicial codes, and governmental policies to be similarly skewed. After all, such proscriptions are all products of the same human brains, with a heaping scoop of provincial influence and self-interest added on top. So, it shouldn't surprise us that these laws and policies often reflect the same ethical miscalculations we as individuals make, including paying disproportionately little attention to failures of inaction.

Consider for example the Ten Commandments, the bedrock of Judaic and Christian religious ethics. The Ten Commandments are largely prohibitive in nature. Eight of them are "thou shall nots," bad actions that are to be avoided.

These are, in order: don't worship other gods, don't make idols, don't take God's name in vain, don't kill, don't commit adultery, don't steal, don't bear false witness against your neighbor, don't covet your neighbor's wife or possessions. Only two of the commandments are "you musts," good actions that if one fails to do (the fourth box), one has committed a sin: keep holy the Lord's day and honor your parents. Since "keep holy the Lord's day" is focused only on honoring the religion itself, just one of the ten commandments is a proactive requirement to do good things for others.

Conversely, the Five Pillars of Islam, the bedrock requirements of that faith, are actually completely proscriptive in nature. They are all requirements to do certain things, with failure to do them (the fourth box) representing moral violations. But much like "keep holy the Lord's day," four of these five "you musts" are focused on honoring the religion itself: declaring there is only one God, Allah, and that Muhammad is his messenger; praying five times a day; making a pilgrimage to Mecca at least once; and fasting during Ramadan. Only one of the five pillars prescribes an action that benefits others, namely—and impressively—a duty to give to charity.

Reading more broadly from the religious holy books, we do come across a number of "dos" in addition to the "don'ts." As discussed earlier, in the Christian Bible's New Testament we see Jesus explicitly directing his followers to do a variety of good actions, including giving what they have to the poor, feeding the hungry, giving clothes to those who need it, visiting the imprisoned, comforting the sick, and so on. The Jewish Tanakh and the Islamic Koran also contain encouragements toward a number of additional "dos" (as well as a plethora of additional "don'ts"). In practice though, the invocations to do good—including the Islamic duty to give to charity and Jesus' directives to help others in need—have generally remained moral nice-to-haves. It is the "thou shall nots," the bad actions, that have commanded the lion's share of moral attention in the major western religions of Christianity, Judaism, and Islam.

A Christian who fails to visit the imprisoned or give to the poor, as directed by Jesus, will virtually never be called to task by his fellow faith members for that failure of inaction. After all, most of his or her fellow faith members are no different. A 2020 study reported by *ChristianityToday.com* found that only 5 percent of church members give regularly to charity. An observant Jew who fails to carry out charitable acts toward others will not fare much worse. And only in countries with the strictest national implementation of Sharia law will Muslims that fail to give the proper amount to charity (the Koran encourages 2.5 percent of wealth above a certain level be donated) face real repercussions. On the other hand, engaging in an action considered bad by a particular religion can result in serious consequences. Punishment can range from the denial of communion and excommunication in Catholicism (and just a few centuries ago imprisonment, torture, and execution in Catholic and Protestant Christian nations) to imprisonment, physical abuse, and execution in certain Muslim nations today.

In summary, if we leave aside proactive requirements on spiritual rituals and beliefs, western religious doctrine and western religious behavior has been overwhelmingly focused on prohibiting and policing bad actions. Failure to do good, including inaction in the face of the preventable suffering of others, has been of comparatively little concern.

Modern legal systems are constructed in much the same way. Nearly all criminal law and the overwhelming majority of civil law consists of prohibitions on doing bad things, be that breaking and entering, assault, murder, theft, and so on.

There are, particularly on the civil law side, some torts and statutes that prohibit and punish certain inactions. But even these statutes are largely meant to prevent bad actions, such as breaking contracts, violating labor laws, or creating unsafe work conditions. What is being guarded against and punished is a failure to live up to commercial agreements or a failure to meet basic standards that were put in place to prevent active harms from occurring. Such laws are not requirements to proactively help those in need.

Outside of paying taxes and caring for dependent family members, citizens have almost no legal or civil obligations to use their resources—be that money, time, energy, or other resources—to help others. English Common Law, which is the legal bedrock in many countries including the United States, imposes no general duty to help others. The only exceptions are when one created a hazardous situation that puts a person in danger in the first place, or when one has a special relationship with the person in peril (for example they are a child or spouse).

There are around two dozen countries—including Germany, France, Tunisia, and Brazil—as well as ten US states which do have so-called "duty to rescue" laws. Such laws generally require citizens who come across another person in distress or danger to try to help, either by intervening directly if it's safe to do so or by contacting authorities. But despite being on the books, such laws are almost never enforced, and most people are not even aware they exist. And even if they were enforced, these laws only apply to situations involving immediate specific physical danger or harm—such as a car crash, fire, or choking incident—and for which a person is physically present (perhaps a case of attentional bias at work). They do not apply to other situations such as long-term ongoing harms, psychologically but not physically harmful situations, or harms that are not happening directly in front of someone. In other words, they do not apply to nearly 100 percent of the situations of human suffering that we have the ability to help resolve or prevent and that will befall others if we don't act.

A person who has the ability to but fails to provide food for a hungry child living in their house, resulting in the child suffering severe malnutrition or starvation, would be condemned by the public and sent to jail for years. A person who has the ability to but fails to provide food for a hungry child living in the street near their house, resulting in the child suffering severe malnutrition or starvation, would not receive so much as a bat of the eye from the public or from authorities. But both situations are identical in terms of ability to act, failure to do so, and the real-world consequences of inaction.

Whether there should be significantly stronger legal duties to help others whom we have the ability to help, and if so how and when such laws should be applied, is a nuanced set of questions that would require a much more protracted discussion. These points around law are not being presented to suggest that there are fast and easy policy solutions that should be enacted. Rather, they are presented to point out that our legal systems, much like western religious codas, reflect and reinforce our tendency to focus almost exclusively on actions, ignoring the incredibly consequential impacts of inaction.

With our internal cognitive biases—biases carved deeply into the grooves of our mental wiring by hundreds of thousands of years of evolutionary selection—directing attention and ethical concern away from the fourth box, and with the rule books of national law and mainstream religious doctrines doing the same, it's easy to understand why most of us have not thought much about the ethics of inaction.

Even if we do stop to think it through carefully, accepting ethical responsibility for the consequences of our inaction is not easy. As you've read this book, your mind has probably been working to formulate reasons why—even though it is the case that there is great suffering in the world and even though action on your part could prevent some of that acute misery for many individuals—you don't have and shouldn't have an ethical duty to act, at least not beyond the current norms of directing a few percentage points of income to charitable causes.

Owning the fourth box, taking responsibility for our inactions just as much as we take responsibility for our actions, is not easy. Would having such an expectation of ourselves be fair? Would it be reasonable? Is it even possible?

CHAPTER FOUR

The
Impossible Standard

*"Apathy...is the erosion of ability
to commit oneself to important
causes, to care deeply about
other people, and to take risks
in the struggle against every
form of human bondage."*
—DANIEL MIGLIORE

The Impossible Standard

On top of the evolutionary and cultural reasons we might not be inclined to think about the ethics of inaction, there are some pretty compelling reasons why we might not *want* to think about it.

When it comes to thinking about and judging others, it's much easier to weigh someone up if you just go by their actions. It's easy to hear about a good or bad thing someone supposedly did and come to a quick decision about their character (a manifestation of at least two cognitive biases, the availability bias and the salience bias, which lead us to jump to conclusions based on information that is immediately present and particularly resonant). As it stands now, our judgments of others already generally ignore the fact that the vast majority of good and bad things any other person does are going to be unknown to us. The idea of also taking the time to factor in the things a person could have done but didn't—their harms of inaction—would make such judgments even more challenging. So, why bother? As we have seen in our discussion of mental heuristics, our brains prefer snap judgments, prioritizing speed over getting things right whenever the personal stakes are not high.

Much more importantly though, focusing only on actions provides a much simpler and easier ethical terrain for thinking about and judging ourselves. When we focus only on our actions and ignore our inactions, 99 percent of our day becomes ethically neutral. When we're watching a movie, taking a walk, hanging out with friends, answering calls at our job, or so on, what we're doing does not seem to have any ethical valence. There could be occasional moments where we feel we did something bad (lost our temper and cursed at a customer) or good (baked a cake to cheer up a friend because they've been feeling down lately), but these are infrequent and relatively trivial, minor blips on an otherwise empty ethical radar screen.

When only a tiny fraction of our day has ethical import, living ethically is much, much easier. We can spend nearly all day ethically zoned out, not needing to pay attention to whether we are doing the right thing or not. Only very occasionally do we have to exercise the self-discipline needed to do the right thing when we don't feel like it, such as forcing ourselves to stay patient with a difficult customer or foregoing a bit of sleep to bake a cake for a friend (to stick with those two admittedly trite examples).

If, on the other hand, we accept that inactions have real-world consequences—and therefore have ethical weight—the picture changes completely. In some sense, every minute of our lives now carries an ethical decision. Choosing to spend an hour watching TV means choosing not to spend that hour helping individuals who badly need help. Similarly, every dollar we spend becomes an ethical decision. Choosing to spend twenty-five dollars going to the movies is choosing to not donate those twenty-five dollars to a family in Bangladesh scraping by on two dollars a day. Even what we do with our thoughts becomes an ethical decision. Mental bandwidth spent on one thing, such as thinking about what we might want to do this weekend, becomes mental bandwidth not spent on something else, such as thinking about how we can better help people in extreme poverty or animals suffering on intensive farms.

When we start to pay attention to the things we don't do in the same way we pay attention to the things we do, and when we keep present in our minds the fact that our inactions have as much of an impact on others as our actions, a world that was largely ethically neutral and therefore able to be navigated with relatively minimal attention and effort becomes saturated with ethical consequence at every turn—requiring far more attention, effort, and sacrifice.

This is very cognitively challenging. It is mentally taxing to remain consistently ethically present. It is mentally taxing to regularly consider and reconsider the things we could be doing with our time and money that would reduce others' suffering.

It is also emotionally challenging. When ethical responsibility is ever-present, the continual weight of that responsibility is a heavy burden to bear. Given there will always be more we could be doing than we will actually do, we run the risk of frequently feeling guilty for not doing enough.

And of course, actually acting on this ethic—trying to turn Good Things We Don't Do into Good Things We Do by putting more of our time, money and energy toward helping those who are suffering—will inevitably require us to make sacrifices, to give up bits of comfort and happiness and personal pleasure, so that other individuals may have their suffering eased.

Owning what we don't do, paying attention to not just our actions but also our inactions, creates an ethical universe that appears too all-pervasive, too ceaselessly demanding for us to successfully navigate cognitively, emotionally, or practically. We become like Sisyphus, forever pushing our massive ethical boulder up a mountain but never able to reach the summit and rest because there is always further to go.

In short, when we accept that our inactions have consequences just as our actions do—and therefore matter ethically just as our actions do—we find ourselves face to face with an impossible ethical standard. Even if we were to spend every waking minute trying to help others, we could always sleep less or figure out how to be more productive with each hour of our time. Even if we were inclined to give away every dollar, we'd have to question whether doing so would indeed result in the most good. And regardless of how altruistically we were spending our time and money, we could always be working more intelligently than we are now, finding more efficient ways to use our time and money to reduce suffering.

How can we accept, let alone embrace, an impossible ethical standard like this one?

Externally, there is little to no incentive to own our inactions. There is no external reason to put significantly more of our resources, time, or mental energy toward helping those who are suffering greatly. We will gain nothing physically—not more comfort, security, possessions, or anything else. We will also gain nothing socially. Almost no one will know that we are making the effort; and for the few people who do know, any polite praise or words of commendation they give will fade into memory almost immediately.

Internally, we may reap some benefits, such as a richer feeling of meaning and purpose in our lives, heightened feelings of self-efficacy, a greater sense of control over our environment, and a heightened sense of drive—all of which can increase our long-term happiness and well-being. But the mind is a flexible thing, and there are other ways to achieve these positive internal benefits without subjecting ourselves to the demanding cognitive and emotional workloads and personal trade-offs that trying to live up to this sort of ethical standard would require.

When it comes to owning our inactions, we will not be rewarded if we do—not physically, not legally, and not socially. We will not be punished if we don't—not physically, not legally, and not socially. And any emotional rewards we may reap can also be found elsewhere, down easier paths.

It may seem foolish, then, to embrace such a standard. It may seem naïve and misguided to think that an ethical standard like this could work in the first place. We might therefore conclude that we should put out of mind the harms that result from our inactions, that we shouldn't hold ourselves to account for the Good Things We Don't Do—other than in particularly exceptional circumstances. To go down that route is to relegate ourselves to significant and ongoing personal sacrifice with no significant personal benefit, only to judge ourselves as not good enough at the end of the day anyway.

And yet...

And yet while we mull on these thoughts, a child sits listlessly on a concrete median in the middle of a road while his brother begs for money from passing cars. While we weigh these considerations in our mind from a comfortable seated position, a mother who must walk four hours a day to get drinkable water for her family is on the road under a hot sun. When we put down this book and walk away, a highly intelligent and curious animal will remain locked for the next four years in a metal crate so small she cannot turn around.

In other words, the realities of the world will not bend to our conclusions of what is fair for us, to our preference for ease and pleasure, or to our desire to feel good about ourselves.

The notion that inaction has consequences for the suffering and well-being of others is a factual proposition. It is not an opinion that can be argued about and dissected yet neither proven nor disproven. It is a factual proposition that can be tested and shown to be either true or false. And leaving aside any mind-bending metaphysical argument, I think we can agree it is a proposition that is true. I think we can agree that when we choose not to do something, our inaction can have consequences in the real world in more or less the same way as our actions have consequences. In both cases, there are other factors at play, and our inaction or action doesn't always make an actual difference. But it often does, and the cause-and-effect link is plainly visible. And as is the case with our actions, in certain cases the real-world consequences of our inactions can be severe.

Accepting this to be true then, the question each of us must answer is how we will choose to live in light of that reality. We can bemoan the situation and take the position that we did not ask for and do not want the responsibility for which it calls, that we do not want the pressure, guilt, or mental and physical sacrifice that responding to it would entail. But regardless of how we feel about it, the reality remains.

Another way to say this would be as follows: Close your eyes and imagine you live in a world where every minute of time you use, every dollar you spend, every bit of mental energy you allocate, could mean the difference between another person living or dying, between another individual suffering intensely or having their suffering relieved. Now open your eyes. You are living in that world. What are you going to do?

Getting Clear on What We Want

Our external response to this question will be reflected in how we choose to live our day-to-day lives given this reality. We might shift our choices of action and inaction a little, a moderate amount, a lot, or not at all. We might decide to direct a little more of our money, time, and mental energy toward the suffering of others, a lot more, or none at all. Before we get to our external response though, let's first talk about our internal mental response.

Our conclusions on what this reality of the world means for us personally—on whether we should have ethical responsibility for what we don't do, whether a standard like this is fair or sensible, whether we should feel a little or a lot or not at all bad about suffering that continues because of our inaction—matters to us internally in the same way that all important conclusions matter. They will influence our sense of the world, how we order and interpret it, and how we feel being alive in it. They will influence our sense of others, be it those we love, those we loathe, those we interact with throughout the course of the day, or those we pass by on the street. They will influence our sense of ourselves, including whether we see ourselves as good or bad, whether we feel guilty or proud or somewhere in between, and whether other beliefs and viewpoints we have held up to this point still seem valid.

In that realm of internal consideration and internal response, it's understandable why one might conclude that the ethical standard presented here is not fair or reasonable and that we shouldn't try to hold ourselves to it. Devotees of ethical philosophy might reach that conclusion using formalized logic or by pointing toward a competing ethical system that makes more sense to them. For most people though, the conclusion that such a standard isn't one we want to strive toward could probably be summed up in this way: "That's too much to ask. I don't want to do it, and I don't want to feel guilty for not doing it."

It's a very understandable response. There certainly are logical reasons to reach that conclusion. And if that's your personal conclusion, this book will not really try to persuade you otherwise. The point of this book is not to make judgments about who is good and who is bad or to say that we have some transcendent moral duty to spend all of our time and money helping others. In fact, the internal conclusions you or I come to on what we should and shouldn't be responsible for and on what ethical standards we should hold ourselves to, aren't

particularly important. That may sound completely counterintuitive, but consider the following.

Let's assume you think through this reality of the world we
live in and land on one of two personal views. Either yes, we
have an ethical duty to try to relieve others' suffering if we can,
and our inactions matter similarly to our actions. Or no, we
have no ethical imperative to help (beyond a modest amount)
those who are suffering, and in general we are only responsible
for our actions.

If your conclusion was yes, great. You've now got a belief,
and perhaps the beginnings of an internal emotional reward
system, that will give you some personal mental payoff from
putting more of your time, money, and energy toward helping
those who are suffering. When you direct more of your resources
toward helping others, you might feel pride or satisfaction from
doing what you believe is right. When you fail to do so, you
might find anxiety or guilt goading you back into action.

And if your conclusion was no, fine. You've got a belief and
internal emotional reward system that tell you there's no general
need to put your time, money, and energy toward helping those
who are suffering. And you won't feel bad or guilty if you don't.

In either case: so what?

As with many viewpoints, the belief as to whether we do
or don't have responsibility for something—whether we should
feel like we're a good or bad person if we do or don't do something—is, in and of itself, an abstract mental game largely
detached from the external world. It's not our internal ethical
beliefs that ultimately affect the lives of those who are suffering;
it's what we do and don't do externally.

Naturally, our ethical beliefs can influence how we act in
the world. But so can many other things. And each one of us

can take the actions that relieve the suffering of others even if we believe we have absolutely no ethical responsibility to do so.

We don't need to believe we *have* to do something or that we *should* do something or that we'll be a bad person if we don't do something to still do it. We can disbelieve any of those things and yet do it anyway because we *want* to do it. We can do it freely, out of pure choice rather than any sense of ethical obligation. A person can absolutely believe that ethically they don't have to, don't need to, should not be expected to, and are just as good a person if they don't put significantly more resources toward those who are suffering and yet still put significantly more resources toward helping those who are suffering, simply because they want to do so.

The same logic also holds if one were to approach this question from the viewpoint of religious morality, for example if you believe in a God and an afterlife and think about this issue with an eye toward what you need to do to make it to a heaven. Here, too, the internal answers you come to are (in a certain sense) irrelevant. If you believe the active encouragement to help those in need peppered into the holy books or traditions of Judaism, Islam, Christianity or any other religion represent real moral requirements to spend our time and money addressing suffering we didn't cause, then great. You can do those things as part of your efforts to secure a comfortable afterlife for yourself. And if you conclude that doing these sorts of things are not requirements to get into a heaven or reincarnate into a higher form or similar, you can still do them anyway. Whatever your religious beliefs may be, it's pretty certain that spending significantly more money, time, and energy helping those who are suffering is not going to violate your religion's principles.

If one doesn't think there's an ethical need to care about the suffering of others or that they bear ethical responsibility for harms that result from their inaction, why might such a person still choose to put significantly more resources, time, and energy toward helping others? They might do so because it brings about a good outcome for others, and that outcome might be something they *want*.

A sense of ethical obligation is one force that can drive attention to the fourth box. Preference can be another. We can desire a world with less suffering just like we might desire spending a relaxing afternoon at the beach. We can prefer a world where other individuals are happier just like we might prefer one flavor of ice cream to another. It isn't just the belief that "I should" but also the feeling that "I want" that can motivate us to act in ways that do great good for others.

And that points toward another critical insight. For many of us, paying attention to the fourth box ultimately means being more deliberate in thinking through what we really want in the world and exercising the self-discipline to act on those preferences. This point is so important and perhaps counter-intuitive that it's worth stating again. For many of us, paying attention to the Good Things We Don't Do ultimately means being more deliberate in thinking through what we really want in the world and exercising the self-discipline to act on those preferences.

This book is certainly not advocating for a self-centric "live your best life" mindset. Quite conversely it is advocating for an increased focus on reducing the suffering of others even when it comes at the expense of our own enjoyment. Nevertheless, for many people, successfully carrying out the ethos of the book can feel like and in certain ways is a type of self-realization exercise, a clarifying of and acting on one's own deeper preferences.

If I have $100 that I don't need to maintain my own basic health and happiness, there are a lot of things I can do with that money. I can take my partner out for a nice dinner and drinks, essentially buying several hours of personal enjoyment for the two of us. Alternatively, I can donate that $100 to a charity that will use it to perform a simple cataract surgery to restore vision to a man in Vietnam who can't afford the surgery and has been living functionally blind for several years. These are two different goods, two different outcomes I can create in the world. Which one do I personally value more? Which one do I have a stronger preference to bring into existence in the world?

It's a similar situation to that faced in the French fries vs. broccoli conundrum, where we are ultimately asking ourselves whether our stronger preference is to have a few minutes of gustatory pleasure or to live a healthier and longer life. If we stopped and thought it through carefully, the latter is probably much more important to us. Maybe not every time; there may be days when we crave the pleasure of eating French fries so much that in that instance, the short-term pleasure really is more important to us. But nine times out of ten, it is probably the broccoli that is more in line with our deeper, big-picture preference to live a longer, healthier, and more mobile life. The challenge lies in keeping our big-picture preferences in mind when making decisions, and having the self-discipline to prioritize them over the immediate wants that evolution has hardwired into us. (In this case, those evolutionary instincts include the bias toward favoring small immediate gains over larger but less immediate ones, and the drive to consume excessive amounts of fat and salt.)

Similarly, for many of us the challenge with owning our inactions and putting significantly more resources, time, and energy toward reducing the suffering of others is not that doing so would be acting in opposition to our own preferences. It's not that doing so would mean giving up something we want for something we don't want. When we stop and reflect on it, we probably do value reducing the suffering of someone in misery more than we value a new car or a dinner out. The challenge is putting in the mental work to think it through, to reflect on our deeper wants and to exercise the self-discipline to prioritize them. In ethics as in eating as in life, we are continually making decisions that are ultimately choices between our big-picture wants and the small momentary wants that are less important to us but incredibly tempting because of their immediate payoff.

The good news is that our minds are very flexible and acclimate reasonably well and reasonably quickly with repetition. Eat healthy for a few months and broccoli starts to taste nearly as delicious as French fries, perhaps even more delicious. Similarly, once we've gotten into a routine of putting more resources toward reducing the suffering of others, doing so can start to bring nearly as much or even more happiness as spending those resources on ourselves. But it takes self-discipline and practice to get there.

We should also keep in mind that with anything we care about and dive deeply into in life—be it a romantic relationship, golf, painting, or doing good for others—our expectation should not be perfection. Perfection is not possible. Perfection is not likely to even be our goal, because with a goal like that, we would have no space left in our days or our minds for other things we also care about or enjoy. Life would be a lot less fun if we never ate a French fry again or if we never spent any money on personal pleasures. Even the world's greatest golfers, painters, and romantic partners did not spend 100 percent of their time on those endeavors, despite the centrality of each in their lives.

In other words, the perfect need not be the enemy of the great. We can agree that factually a perfectly healthy diet would never include fries, and we may aspire to be eat very healthily, but that doesn't mean the goal or expectation we would set for ourselves would be never eating junk food. A more realistic goal, and one that best reflected our deeply considered preferences, might be for healthy options to be the default and junk food the very occasional exception. The same holds true for focusing more of our resources on helping those who are severely suffering. After we've met our own basic needs, having our default use of money be helping others, with discretionary spending on ourselves the exception, would be an admirable approach. It would also be an approach that for a good number of us is in line with our big-picture preferences and what we truly value.

For the blind woman who can see again, the malnourished child who gets enough food to be able to return to school and resume learning, or the animal spared from a lifetime of torturous conditions, the exact constellation of our internal motivations for giving more of our money, time or energy—whether it came from a sense of ethical responsibility or was simply a freely chosen expression of personal preference—does not matter. The fact that like them we are not and never will be perfect people does not matter either.

And if it doesn't matter to those who are suffering greatly, then it need not concern us either. We need not be hung up on whether we do or don't have ethical responsibility to help those who are suffering. We need not be hung up on the fact that paying attention to our inactions the way we pay attention to our actions presents a standard of perfection that is impossible to attain. When we strip away the swirl of internal beliefs on responsibility, fairness, guilt, goodness, badness, and so on and when we look just at the real-world consequences our actions and inactions have for others, the picture turns from cloudy to clear, from threatening to empowering.

Judgment

When it comes to that swirl of internal considerations on good and bad, on right and wrong, it's also worth taking a few moments to consider our judgments of others in light of what's been discussed so far.

Public moral praise and public moral approbation have been a part of modern societies since such societies sprang into existence, and likely extend far back on our evolutionary tree. Behavioral studies show that even chimps and monkeys have a sense of fairness and of what behaviors are acceptable and unacceptable and that they will express outrage and punish or ostracize others that act out of line—the simian equivalent of moral approbation.

What is considered praiseworthy and what is considered damnable (and how damnable), however, has continually shifted over time. And it can also vary just as much between two different cultural or political pockets of a given country as it can between two different continents or historical eras. But regardless of the historical period and the particular culture, and regardless of whether it is praise or approbation, public moralizing has almost always focused on the same two boxes that we as individuals focus on when considering our own ethics: good things that were done and bad things that were done. Inactions and the consequences of those inactions receive virtually no attention and almost never generate public moral approbation or praise.

When we consider, though, that today the consequences of inactions are often far worse than the consequences of actions, the moral landscape of good and bad, of what might deserve praise and why and what might deserve criticism and why, shifts dramatically. Those who are criticized may well deserve criticism—but less for their attention-grabbing bad acts and more for their failures of inaction which we have not considered. Those who are highly praised may not be worthy of the esteem they're being given once we reflect on their own failures of inaction. Considering others' inactions alongside their actions gives us a more well-rounded perspective on them and can also likely lead to more productive public discourse.

To use an example that may seem extreme, consider Jeffrey Epstein. In 2019, the billionaire was arrested on numerous counts of sex trafficking and related charges for reportedly having dozens of underage girls transported across state and country lines to provide him with sexual services. Some of the victims of Epstein's actions spoke out publicly about the long-lasting emotional impact those experiences had on them. Public condemnation was swift and vigorous, with newspaper headlines across the country decrying Epstein as monstrous. Television programs were quickly packaged together to walk viewers step by sordid step through Epstein's life and crimes.

The harm caused by his inactions, by his failure to use his extravagant wealth to help those in desperate need, was wholly absent from the public moral condemnation. Some media coverage did criticize Epstein's lavish lifestyle, which included owning his own mega-yacht and private island. But criticism in this area centered on the ostentatious nature of his spending, and how his level of wealth may have led him to feel he was above the law; it was not about the harms that resulted to real people because he failed to share resources with those in need.

As much harm as Epstein caused to the dozens of people that were trafficked, there is something else that is also true: the amount of suffering that people endured as a result of Epstein's inactions was far, far, far greater. As a result of Epstein's actions, dozens of women experienced significant and ongoing emotional pain and damage. That is condemnable. As a consequence of Epstein's inactions—his failure to share his great wealth— hundreds of thousands of people continued to endure intense suffering. Tens of thousands of people died. What Epstein did led to real pain and suffering in the world. What he failed to do led to exponentially more real pain and suffering in the world.

It can be hard to view things this way because it might feel that by broadening our scope of attention, we lose focus on those his actions hurt—real people with specific names, faces and stories, several of whom were quoted in the press. Further, his actions were way outside of the bounds of the normal (even when it comes to criminal activity), and the salacious nature of the charges on a hot button social issue were enough to trigger revulsion. These elements—which capture our attention by triggering the Identifiable Victim Effect, Attention Bias, Salience Bias and Affect Heuristic—make it easy to empathize with the victims' pain, which of course we should. But those who suffered as a consequence of Epstein's inactions are also real people with specific names, faces and stories, just ones we have not seen or heard.

Whether we look just at Epstein's bad actions, or at both his actions and inactions, we are likely to come to the same basic conclusion: he is someone whose choices likely led to far more harm and suffering in the world than good. But looking at the broader landscape of consequences brought about by his choices, including his ongoing decision not to use his vast wealth to help those in need, gives us a more complete picture. Having that more complete picture can help us stay on guard against similar failings in our own lives, and against similar problems in society in general.

While Epstein is an easy villain, we can also apply the same lens to those who are relatively beloved. Take, for example, Oprah Winfrey. There is a laundry list of good things Oprah has done, including according to public reports donating at least $200 million to charitable efforts. It's hard to name a celebrity more universally well-regarded than she. And it's specifically because she has done so many good things and is so beloved that it's useful to consider the consequences of her inactions, the Good Things She Didn't Do, in the same way we examined those of Epstein.

Oprah's personal purchases over the years are reported to have included the following: a $42 million Bombardier Global Express private plane; a $52 million mansion in Santa Barbara (into which she subsequently put tens of millions of dollars in renovations); a $28 million horse farm in Montecito; a $14 million home in Telluride with a fifty-six-foot wine tunnel, heated driveway, custom-made $70,000 bathtub, and fiber-optic lighted glass bridge; a $60 million estate in Hawaii; a private library valued at over $1.5 million; and millions of dollars' worth of personal automobiles, including a $2.5 million Mercedes Benz.

The real-world consequence of Winfrey's decisions to make these types of personal luxury purchases instead of using that wealth in a different way is that tens of thousands of people have suffered or died. This would have been prevented had Oprah instead donated that money to efficient charities. The ongoing suffering and death of thousands more is a direct consequence of choices of inaction Winfrey continues to make daily. When it comes to inaction in the face of great need despite great ability to help, Oprah (like Epstein) is a John Pierre on steroids.

With that in mind, when we consider not just the consequences of Oprah's actions but also the consequences of her inactions, would we still consider her to be someone deserving of the strong public moral admiration she enjoys (distinct from the admiration she receives for being a great talk show host or businessperson)?

The goal here is not to point a finger of reproach at the uber-rich. There are others who have developed fortunes as vast as Winfrey or Epstein and who are working to carefully, methodically deploy the vast bulk of their wealth over time toward efforts that do great good, with Bill Gates and Dustin Moskovitz being two prominent examples among others. And most people in the industrialized world, whether they fall on the upper, middle, or lower range of the income spectrum—and whether they are lovable like Oprah, detestable like Epstein, or somewhere in between—would fail the same type of critique we have just levied against those two. The difference would be one of magnitude—the ability to help dozens or hundreds versus the ability to help tens of thousands—but not of kind.

The point is that we should think more carefully about whether someone is worthy of criticism or worthy of praise, and why. Water-cooler narratives on such things can already wildly miss the mark, and this is doubly the case when we consider a person's inactions in addition to their actions. This is true not just for public figures but also the regular people in our own lives: our neighbors, coworkers, family members, and friends. It's also true for ourselves. The unavoidable truth is that there are many people in the world who are suffering intensely or who have died as a consequence of the Good Things We Didn't Do.

That realization should leave us with a healthy dose of humility, particularly when we feel inclined to judge others. We can thump our chests in outrage over a tweet a politician, comedian, or everyday airline flight attendant wrote, but is the suffering that will result from that one tweet anything remotely close to the suffering that has resulted because of our own inaction in failing to use more of our time, money, and energy to help those suffering in preventable misery? When professional pundits on television or armchair pundits on social media take pains to emphasize how unforgivably racist (for example) they think a certain statement was, it is worth considering how much suffering individuals of that particular skin color, or any skin color, have endured because of the pundit's own failure to put a greater portion of their money, time, and energy toward helping them. In most cases, the suffering that is happening in the world as a result of the inaction of the condemner is far worse than the suffering that may result from the words or actions of the one being condemned.

That's not to say we shouldn't criticize things we think are bad. But the humility and self-awareness that come from recognizing that we ourselves are not beyond reproach—that others have suffered greatly in the past and are suffering greatly right now as a consequence of our own failures of inaction—might dampen the hyperbole and holier-than-thou attitudes that derail productive public discourse. Such self-awareness might incline us to direct our criticisms in a more reasonable tone and in a more pragmatic manner, focusing on explaining why we disagree with specific actions and policies rather than on demonizing specific people or groups.

Addressing the fourth box, the Good Things We Don't (Yet) Do, starts with realizing the consequences of our inactions and reflecting on our higher-order preferences for what we want in the world. But understanding and believing in the importance of owning our inactions is just the first step. Putting our new belief into action is another thing entirely. We will turn now in the second half of this book to the practical matter of doing just that: exploring the nuts and bolts of what owning our inactions entails, as well as methods we can use to increase our drive and ability to do great good.

PART II

THE DRIVE TO DO MORE

CHAPTER FIVE

Owning What
We Don't Do

*"He who would accomplish little
must sacrifice little; he who would
achieve much must sacrifice
much; he who would attain
highly must sacrifice greatly."*
—JAMES ALLEN

Money, Time, and Mental Energy

So, how do we do it? If we want to own the fourth box, if we want to turn Good Things We Don't Do into Good Things We Do, how should we approach such an effort?

Throughout this book, we've referenced three key resources each of us has that can be used to help others: money, time, and mental energy. Let's look at each of those in turn, starting with money.

It's obvious that money is a critical resource, and for that reason, this book has focused primarily on what we do with our money. But it's worth considering just why money is so powerful.

Money is, of course, a relatively recent invention. Originally, goods and labor were shared collectively within small tribal groups. As early civilizations arose, barter-based economies began to emerge. The shift from barter-based economies to the use of standardized currencies (such as money) allowed resources to begin to be stored and utilized in ways that had never previously been possible.

For one thing, the use of a standardized currency made it easier to procure and direct the time of others. By time, we mean here the time that others would be willing to spend laboring on something. Buying others' time can mean paying for services, like hiring a chef to prepare us food or a mechanic to fix our car. But even buying physical goods is ultimately paying for someone else's time or, more accurately, paying for small bits of time from many people. The purchase price of a loaf of bread includes small payments to a grocery store stocker for spending time putting the bread on the shelf, a clerk for spending time ringing up the sale, a truck driver for spending time delivering the loaf, a farmer for spending time growing the wheat, and so on.

The use of standardized currency also ultimately greased the wheels of specialization. Instead of everyone learning to bake their own bread, build their own house, teach their own children, and so on, currency allowed individuals to specialize in a particular area and then easily exchange the fruits of that specialty for the fruits of others' specialties. Over time, the quality of goods and services rose dramatically thanks to the growing expertise that specialization allowed.

Specialization combined with growing societies and the ease with which currency can be stored and exchanged also allowed work to be done at increasingly larger scales, resulting in greater efficiency and lower costs. Today, using money to pay others to do something for us almost always gets us a higher quality, faster, and cheaper result than if we were to do that thing ourselves. Consider the amount of time it would take to create a loaf of bread yourself, starting with growing and harvesting the wheat, building an oven, and so on. Having specialists (farmers, millers, bakers, and so on) do the work for you and tens of thousands of other customers at the same time creates a world where you and everyone else can procure a loaf of bread far more quickly, cheaply, and easily than would have been the case had you created it yourself.

The same holds true when it comes to using our resources to reduce the suffering of others. We can try to do the work directly with our own hands and our own time. But unless we are particularly specialized in and knowledgeable about one of the most cost-effective ways of helping those in need, doing it directly is not likely to be very efficient. Just as the most efficient way to get a loaf of bread is to pay those with specialization and scale to produce it for us, if we want an animal spared from misery, a child spared from an abusive household, or a man provided with life-preserving medicine he can't afford, the most efficient way to get that outcome is usually to pay those with specialization and, in some cases, scale to produce that result for us. This is what we are doing when we donate to effective charities.

Specialization and scale, along with technological advancement, have allowed the costs of certain consumer goods and services to drop dramatically. Even a minimum wage American worker can earn enough in ten minutes to buy a loaf of bread that would have taken her days or months to produce directly herself. Similarly, specialization, technological advancements and smart strategy, combined in some cases with scale, allow a handful of charities to produce a huge amount of good for a shockingly modest cost. Real examples of this include charitable programs that prevent one death from malaria for every several thousand dollars donated, restore vision to someone through cataract surgery for roughly every one hundred dollars donated, or spare several dozen animals from a lifetime of particularly cruel treatment for each single dollar donated. As a result, even a minimum wage American worker can earn enough in ten minutes to spare numerous animals from a lifetime of suffering—something they almost surely could not have achieved in the same period of time had they tried to do it directly.

As these examples suggest, time spent directly helping others is usually less productive. Naturally there are exceptions, and there are some areas where authentic and unpaid social connection is what is most needed—for example supporting those facing mental health issues due to loneliness or isolation. But in most cases, volunteering is akin to baking a loaf of bread ourselves. If we want to enjoy the process of baking bread, great, that's a good reason to bake it. But if our goal is not the personal pleasure of baking, but rather just wanting to efficiently get a loaf of bread to eat, we're much better off using our money to buy it from the store.

Similarly, using our time to directly help others can be a great way to enjoy the good feelings that come from doing something positive. Studies consistently show that volunteering increases our feelings of happiness and well-being. And volunteering is certainly better for the world than not doing anything altruistic with that time. But if our goal is not personal pleasure but rather efficiently reducing the suffering of others, we're much more efficient when we use our money to pay the best specialists to do it for us. Naturally if we don't have money and don't have any way to get money (such as by working), paying specialists to do it for us isn't an option. But if you're reading this book, chances are you earn or are able to earn a significant (or quite significant) amount of money by global standards.

Another key difference between time and money is the even distribution of time and the uneven distribution of money. Everyone has twenty-four hours in the day. We can try to be more efficient with how we use our time but we cannot stockpile it, so we'll never have more hours in the day than anyone else. Money, on the other hand, can be conserved and aggregated. As a result, money is unevenly distributed, with huge disparities in individual wealth within communities and across the world. The ability to stockpile money, and those large disparities in wealth, make money a powerful lever for change.

Because of these differences, marginal amounts of our money can do huge good in ways that marginal amounts of our time cannot. A janitor earning the minimum wage in the United States could pick up two extra shifts over a weekend, donate what he earned from that weekend to an efficient charity, and effectively restore vision to someone who has lost it. Alternatively, that janitor could work two extra shifts each week for a month and then donate what he earned from those to a charity that passed the money directly on to the global poor. If he did so, he would double the annual income of a poor family, providing them with more food, medicine, and warmth or giving them the ability to plant a new field of crops or start a new business. If, instead, that janitor was to spend the same amount of time volunteering directly for one of these causes, it would be all but impossible for him to achieve anywhere close to that amount of good.

There are, however, several important ways in which our time can be used to do a great deal of good, and one of those is captured in the example just given. We can use our time to make more money and then use that money to help those who are suffering.

Most of us have numerous ways we could make more money: increasing the number of hours we work at our current job, shifting to a different job with higher pay, taking on a side job, and so on. Perhaps the reason we don't work a few more hours per week now is that the extra pay we'd get from it is not that important to us. In weighing an extra hundred dollars against a few extra hours of free time each week, we've chosen the free time. But when we consider what we could do for others with the money we could earn from those additional hours, our thinking may shift. Now the choice is not between a few extra hours of free time and having an extra hundred dollars, it is between a few extra hours of free time and being able to give someone their vision back. That may shift our thinking on how many hours we're willing to work.

Considered in that way, time can be a very powerful resource for reducing the suffering of others, albeit indirectly. This is true for everyone, but it is particularly true for those who are in or who could put themselves in a position where they can turn their time into significant financial resources. This includes those who are already in high-income roles and those with the background or skill set to be able to work in high-salary roles.

There is also a second way in which time can potentially be quite valuable. When we noted that using our time to volunteer is in most cases going to be far less efficient than donating our money, that comment was referencing volunteering as it's typically done: spending a few hours each week or each month assisting with an existing charitable effort. But we can also use our time in a much more comprehensive way by taking a non-profit, for-profit, or government job where we can do direct good throughout the course of our day instead of just around the edges of it.

Here, how valuable our time is will be wholly dependent on how hard-working, talented, and smart we are in our work. If we apply for and are offered a position that can do a lot of good, the value of our time there is a function of how much more effective we are in the role than the person who would have taken the job if we hadn't. If the person who was second in line for the job would have performed about the same as us, then there is really no value to the time we spend there. If the person who was second in line for the job would have done it better than us, our use of time in holding the job would actually be harmful. If, on the other hand, our performance would be a lot better than the person who was second in line, our time spent carrying out the role could be very valuable if the work is high-impact. And the more responsibility the position entails, the more valuable our use of time there could be.

There can also be very high value in using our time to create an effective new entity or program that otherwise would not exist. Examples include starting a new non-profit or for-profit company or persuading a government, for-profit or non-profit, to launch an effective new program. As was the case with taking a job that does direct good, the key question here will be what our initiative is replacing. If we create a new charity that simply draws donations away from similar existing charities, and our charity is not more efficient than those others, the time we spend on the effort is not generating any real value. If our charity is less efficient than those it pulls resources away from, we could ultimately be causing harm. The same holds true for launching new companies in the for-profit sector and initiating new programs in the government sector.

Whenever our time or money are used in ways that affect others' use of resources, the question of whether we are creating more good in the world, having no impact, or causing harm isn't just a function of the direct results we bring about. It's also a function of what we're replacing, of what doesn't happen because others' money or time has been directed toward our endeavor instead.

As is probably clear by now, the resources of money and time are strongly intertwined. Money can secure others' time, which (thanks to specialization and scale) can result in more good being done than had we used our time to do good directly. Time can likewise be used to secure money, which in turn can be used for good. Time can also be used to develop specialization in doing good directly through a full-time career or the creation of a new endeavor.

Mental energy, the third resource that each of us has, plays an important and interrelated role as well. When we use money to secure others' time, in addition to securing their physical labor during that time, we're also securing at least some of their mental energy. When we use our own time to make money or to do good directly, we are also putting our own mental energy to work. But the most fundamental and important use of mental energy is the effort we spend thinking through how we can more efficiently use our money and time to help others, and how we can secure more money and time to use toward those ends. This cognitive work—the iterative process of deliberating, testing, learning, and questioning how to both maximize and optimize our money and time for doing good in the world—is what we are mainly referring to when we use the term mental energy in this book. And the amount of mental energy we bring to bear is incredibly consequential.

The unfortunate reality is that most charities, programs, impact-generating businesses, and government programs are incredibly inefficient at reducing suffering and improving well-being. As noted earlier, within the non-profit world, the particularly effective charitable programs are ten thousand times more cost-effective than other programs. We would likely find similarly wide disparities when comparing different government programs or different impact-generating businesses. As a result, if we allocate just a small fraction of our mental energy toward investigating, thinking through, and better understanding how to most efficiently reduce the suffering of others, the good we are able to bring about in the world will be minimal. Allocating only a small fraction of our mental energy toward this area is just as, if not even more, limiting than allocating only a small fraction of our money toward it.

Do we end up using our money on something that reduces the suffering of a large number of individuals or just a few? Do we end up spending our time doing something that has an outsized impact on reducing the misery of others or no impact whatsoever? The outcome will depend in large part on how much mental energy we expend thinking through the best uses of the limited time and money we have, including the indirect impacts, trade-offs, and alternatives to any particular decision. If we don't put in the significant and ongoing cognitive work required to make smart decisions, then no matter how generous we are with our money or time, those resources will largely go to waste. We might give away nearly every dollar we have or spend nearly every waking moment engaged in something that seems good and yet still achieve very little for others. By failing to contribute enough of the critical resource of our mental energy, we would have squandered our resources of money and time.

If we want to have a significant impact on reducing the suffering of others, neither spending money nor spending time are sufficient on their own. It is only with the addition of an equally large investment of mental energy that we can fully own the fourth box and turn the Good Things We Don't Do into (Truly) Good Things We Do.

Making Deliberate Choices in a Zero-Sum Game

Money, time and mental energy are the key resources each of us has at our disposal to reduce the suffering of others. There are two things we can do in regard to those resources to better achieve that goal. We can maximize, increasing the amount of those resources we have available to us. And we can optimize, directing a larger portion of those resources toward things that efficiently reduce suffering.

Increasing the amount of resources we have is incredibly powerful. When we grow the pie, we automatically increase the amount of good we're able to do. And with every bit that we grow the pie, any gains we make in efficiency will go even further. For example, if we become twice as efficient with our money, then we will generate twice the impact. If we become twice as efficient with our money while also tripling the amount of money available to us, we'll generate six times the impact.

When it comes to maximizing resources, time is an area where we can make only modest gains. As we can't add hours to the day, and reducing sleep beyond a modest amount causes a significant drop in productivity and health, the only way to add more time is to live longer. That's certainly a great goal to have, although realistically the most we can hope for with healthy living is expanding our lifespans a mere 10 to 20 percent. That said, the extra 10 to 20 percent could be particularly valuable as it would come at the time in our lives where we've accumulated the most wisdom and perhaps the greatest ability to earn resources with which to do good. Consider, for example, that Warren Buffet earned 99.7 percent of his wealth after the age of fifty-two and 95 percent of his wealth after the age of sixty-five. The prospect that we could achieve similarly sizable success in helping others late in our lives gives good reason to try to live as long as possible.

Our storehouse of mental energy can be increased a bit more than our time. Studies suggest there are various things we can do to increase our mental stamina and clarity, including eating a healthier diet, being more physically active, meditating, doing cognitively demanding exercises, learning new skills, and so on. We'll speak more about building cognitive strength later.

Lastly, increasing the amount of money we have available to us is a very straightforward exercise. We can work to increase our income and wealth in various ways, or alternately, we can try to persuade others to give more of their wealth to programs that do great good. Here, the gap between the amount of money we have now and the amount of money we could have in the future is quite large. While we can only increase the number of hours available to us by 10 to 20 percent and our mental energy by, at best, a few multiples, many of us have the potential to increase the amount of financial resources we have available to us by a magnitude of ten, one hundred, one thousand, or even more.

Although maximizing the amount of resources we have is incredibly important, discussions on how to do so—how to live longer, how to eat a diet that will boost mental functioning, how to earn more, how to fundraise effectively, and so on—are book-length topics unto themselves. They are also topics that have already been covered well by other authors. Therefore, rather than further discussing how to maximize the resources we have—as critical as that is—we'll focus more on how we can optimize our use of those resources to reduce suffering.

How we use the money, time, and mental energy we have is largely a zero-sum game. One hundred dollars spent on a new pair of shoes is one hundred dollars that can't be put toward ending serious animal abuse or preventing female genital mutilation. Eight hours spent playing video games are eight hours that can't be spent earning more money to provide additional food to a family living on two dollars a day. Mental energy spent thinking through what we're going to cook for dinner tonight is mental energy not spent thinking through how we can more effectively help those in dire need. Directing more of our money, time, and mental energy toward those in extreme suffering will always mean we have less of those resources available for other things, including things that bring us enjoyment, comfort, or other personal benefits.

Consider money, a particularly powerful resource and the one that is easiest to quantify. It is easy to point as we did earlier to the extravagant purchases of the rich and famous, the million-dollar cars and private jets, and reflect on how blatantly unnecessary those things are in a world with such dire poverty and other terrible problems that money can help solve. But as the expression goes, when we point out that very real problem, three fingers point firmly back at us. The billion or so people living on two dollars a day and the couple billion that live on a few thousand dollars per year could look up the economic ladder and levy at us more or less the same criticism that we levied on the Oprahs and Epsteins of the world. Like them, we spend much of our money on relatively frivolous goods and pleasures, purchases that likely appear quite wasteful to those living on a dollar a day. Our purchases may be different in scale from Oprah and Epstein, but they are often quite similar in kind.

It probably doesn't feel like most of our spending is wasteful, or even discretionary. It probably feels like necessities such as housing, food, and transportation already eat up most of our budgets. But the basic costs of procuring nutritious food, warm shelter to protect us from the elements, clothes to keep us warm, transportation to get us to and from work, and basic health and hygiene supplies are actually relatively low, a small fraction of the average income in higher-income countries. What we choose to spend on these categories, however, is typically a far higher amount. The gap between the basic cost of these necessities and the amount we actually spend reflects our desire for high-quality versions of each of these things—beautiful, comfortable, convenient, and status-signifying versions. For those of us living in higher-income countries, most of what we are paying for in these categories is not the basic necessity but the premium quality layered on top. In other words, most of what we are paying for is pleasure.

It is the pursuit of that pleasure that often leads things like housing, transportation, and food to occupy a large part of our annual expenses. This includes trying to buy physical pleasure (a tasty meal at a restaurant instead of a healthy but simple meal at home), comfort (a nice and large apartment or house in a nice part of town filled with various accoutrements instead of a small apartment or house in a low-income neighborhood), convenience (a new car instead of relying on buses, bikes, and trains), aesthetic pleasure (a well-appointed house, meals at nicely-appointed restaurants, and stylish clothes instead of more basic versions of each), status (more expensive housing, cars, clothing, and so on), and similar niceties.

On top of these purchases sit our completely discretionary expenses, in which we attempt to buy pleasure through things like novel experiences (travel, new hobbies), temporary entertainment (movies, TV, magazines), status symbols (nice watches, jewelry, the latest iPhone), and so on. Taken altogether, most people in higher-income countries spend the majority of their money—and typically the large majority of it—on personal pleasures as opposed to basic necessities.

It may not feel that we have an abundance of money or that we are spending the large majority of our income on discretionary spending aimed at pleasure and comfort, but this is the result of a quirk of human psychology. Studies show that we take a very narrow perspective when it comes to wealth: we tend to only compare ourselves to those who are doing similar or better than us economically and not to those who are poorer than us or who are extremely poor. And as incomes rise, our standards and expectations rise as well.

For example, although wealth and purchasing power (accounting for inflation) have both increased very significantly in the US since the 1950s, and have generally been increasing year over year for the past seventy years, the percentage of Americans who report they are barely making ends meet is virtually unchanged from where it was in the 1950s. Our standard of living and our expectations have gotten so high that is hard for us to tease out actual human necessities from the luxuries built on top of them. A nice house or apartment, nice car, and significant disposable income for dining and entertainment with friends have come to be viewed as necessities for many people in higher-income countries.

The cost difference between satisfying a basic need and satisfying a basic need with slightly increased personal pleasure layered on top can be a large one. Consider, for example, a couple going out to a moderately nice restaurant for dinner. Between appetizers, food, drinks, taxes and tip, the final bill might be eighty dollars. The alternative, making a simple but tasty meal together at home, might cost ten dollars in groceries. The seventy-dollar difference is the additional pleasure the couple is expecting to get from eating out. It is seventy dollars spent not on meeting nutritional needs but on something else. That could be the gustatory pleasure of particularly delicious food, the novelty of being in different surroundings, the feeling of connection that might come from enjoying the experience together, or something else.

Certainly all of those are good things, and it's quite understandable why we'd want them. But as with all expenditures made for personal pleasure, it's worth keeping in mind what else that seventy dollars could procure. Directed in the right way it could feed a poor family in another country for a month.

It could double that month's salary for one of the billion people around the world who live on two dollars a day, giving them the ability to have warmer clothes, more watertight shelter, more food for two months, or perhaps a pair of eyeglasses. It could spare hundreds of animals the misery of spending a lifetime confined in a tiny cage. Seventy dollars saved per meal could, over the course of several meals, be used to prevent a child from dying of malaria or another tropical disease.

If we want to address the fourth box and take responsibility for our inactions as well as our actions, it's helpful to get clear on just how much of our current spending consists of discretionary expenditures made for our own pleasure. Doing so can allow us to reflect on exactly what it is we are trying to buy—comfort, novelty, connection, gustatory pleasure, or so on—and whether there are other ways to get that same pleasure at a lower cost. Simultaneously, we can keep in mind other things that same amount of money can buy that we also value, such as reducing the suffering of others. Thinking through our spending in this way, we can make decisions that better align with our big picture wants while still giving us much of the personal pleasure we're seeking.

For example, a couple might realize they can have nearly as tasty a meal with just as much novelty and personal connection by cooking a new recipe together at home or by having a picnic in the park. They could then set aside the seventy dollars they saved to buy something else they highly value: a better life for someone in great need.

Thinking about our spending in this way is not only likely to help us reduce a great deal more suffering in the world, it is also liable to leave us better off personally. It can help steer us to do more of the things that really add to our enjoyment of life (many of which have little to no cost) and fewer of the things that we think will make us happier but don't or that provide a trivial amount of enjoyment at a significant cost. A tremendous amount of money—money that if directed in a different way could end an enormous amount of very real suffering—is spent each year on things that we ostensibly buy for our own benefit but that really won't benefit us or add to our happiness at all.

That doesn't mean we'll never be in a position to make a sacrifice. There are plenty of things money can buy that would give us very real enjoyment. For those, we'll have to decide in each instance what we value more: the personal pleasure or the outcome the same amount of money could achieve for someone in dire need. Sometimes, we may choose to forgo the pleasure, acknowledging that we've got it pretty good and, ultimately, we'd rather give someone their vision back than get to enjoy a live concert. Other times, we may go ahead and prioritize our own happiness.

Again, our personal goal is probably not to be completely altruistic at all times. Even if it were, perfection is impossible. But taking a more deliberative approach to what we spend money on, and always keeping in mind the alternate outcomes the money could achieve, will take us a long way toward owning our inactions. Instead of spending money on ourselves ten times out of ten, we might end up sometimes going ahead with the expense, sometimes doing something similar that costs a lot less and generates nearly as much (if not more) happiness, and sometimes forgoing the expense entirely (even though it does mean forgoing a bit of pleasure), with the money we save being directed toward those who need it most.

We face a similar zero-sum game when considering how to use our key resource of time.

As we've discussed, time is an evenly distributed resource and a very limited one. While in some parts of the world work hours have been decreasing, leading to a gradual increase in available free time, in the United States and some other places the average number of hours worked per week has been trending upward. For some people who work long hours, discretionary time (in other words, free time) can be a scarce and personally precious resource.

Some of the things we spend time on are real necessities: procuring food, sleeping, maintaining basic hygiene, exercising to stay healthy, and so on—not to mention, of course, working to earn what we need to meet those basic needs. When it comes to free time, our default approach is to spend it doing things we think will give us pleasure. Our plan for a Sunday afternoon might be relaxing at home watching a movie, going to visit family members, or driving to the beach. As is the case with money, owning what we don't do with our time involves thinking more carefully about what else we could be doing with that time

We discussed earlier how spending our time directly on efforts to do good is usually not particularly efficient, other than exceptional cases where volunteering for a particular program does have an outsized impact or situations where we have the specialized knowledge needed to do highly effective direct charitable work. As a result, if we want to put more of our time toward reducing suffering, the best way to do so is probably to use that time to make more money—which can, in turn, be directed to effective charitable programs.

In other words, effectively giving more of our time likely boils down to working more. That might be as straightforward as working extra hours each week at our current job and directing the marginal money we earn toward helping those who are in desperate need. It could be through adding a side job or another money-making endeavor around the margins of our existing job. It could be working on getting other people to donate or otherwise direct more of their financial resources toward high-impact endeavors. (If we can generate more money from an hour of fundraising than we can from an extra hour of paid work, that approach could be even better; it could also have positive knock-on effects if the people we motivate to donate continue doing so in the future).

Giving more of our time might also look like seeking out another job or another career where we can earn significantly more and then shifting all our working hours toward that more lucrative opportunity. For those who work at charities, socially impactful businesses, or government agencies, giving more of one's time might simply look like putting in longer hours to have a bigger impact with that work.

As is the case with giving more of our money, using more of our time to help those in great need means we will have fewer hours left to spend on our own enjoyment. It's possible that the additional work we add to our plates could be nearly as enjoyable as how we would have spent our free time anyway. If our job is pleasant enough, the extra hours we work may be pleasant enough as well. If we have a side business that we find personally engaging, we might get nearly as much pleasure working on that on a Saturday morning as we would from sleeping in and having a leisurely breakfast. At other times, though, spending more of our free time working will not add to our enjoyment. In those instances, we will have a real choice between personal pleasure and doing something that is not particularly enjoyable but that will greatly benefit others in need.

In addition to giving more of the free time we have available now, we can also think about how to get more of it—shaving off unnecessary time wasters to free up extra minutes and hours with which we can do good. We spoke earlier about how skipping an eighty-dollar dinner out and donating the seventy dollars we saved could have a shockingly large impact on the world, such as helping restore someone's vision or sparing hundreds of animals from a lifetime of acute misery. It's incredible that saving small amounts of money like this can have such a major impact for an individual in need. And since time can be used to make money, it's also the case that small but routinized timesavers can give us the ability to help many more individuals.

Imagine, for example, that we typically make lunch for ourselves and that it takes about fifteen minutes to prepare our lunch each day. If we switch to lunch options that take just five minutes to prepare, we'll save roughly an hour of time each week. If we then turn that time saved into an extra hour of paid work, either at our job or some other income-generating activity, it would result in an extra fifty or so paid hours per year. Depending on our earning potential, this one minor time-saving tweak could allow us to restore vision to fifteen, thirty, or even fifty more people per year or to prevent a child or two from dying of a tropical disease. Would you ever have believed that choosing quicker-to-prepare lunches could create that sort of impact for others? The same principle holds true for any other way in which we can streamline necessary parts or eliminate unnecessary parts of our daily and weekly routines.

It's also worth noting that in our example, we are not turning fifty hours of super-enjoyable leisure time into fifty hours of work drudgery. We are replacing fifty hours of unpaid, mundane work (putting together our meals) with fifty hours of paid (and possibly mundane) work. If preparing lunch happens to be a very pleasurable activity for you as opposed to a ho-hum chore, this example may not apply to you. But we all have mundane elements to our routines that we would do just as well without and which, with minor tinkering, we could streamline or eliminate.

Almost all of us will spend a meaningful portion of our week on work and personal chores we need to do to sustain ourselves. And we will all spend some time doing things for personal enjoyment. But if we keep in mind the outcomes for others that we're able to produce with our time, look for ways to give ourselves more free time, and put a larger portion of that free time toward efforts that can have a big impact (primarily through generating more money), we will be able to relieve far more suffering in the world, turning Good Things We Don't Do into Good Things We Do.

Lastly, we have mental energy. Mental energy is foundational to and critical for doing good, just as it is foundational to and critical for doing anything successfully. If we spend more mental energy thinking about others' pain and our ability to help them, we will be more likely to take action to help them. If we spend more mental energy deliberating on how we can increase the amount of money or time we have available to us, we will be more likely to figure out ways to increase our stock of those resources. And if we spend more mental energy thinking through the best uses of our money and time, we will be more likely to use them efficiently in helping individuals in great need. Our use of mental energy is rather different from our use of money and time. It is not so much a separate category from money and time as it is a resource that we bring to bear in greater or lesser amounts in our deliberations and decisions on how to use our money and time.

Research shows we use that mental energy in two different ways: through nonfocused wandering thought and through concentrated task-oriented thought. These have been called the daydreaming and executive functions of our brain, and each plays an important role in assimilating information and organizing our understanding of the world.

Our wandering, nonfocused mental energy is deployed in a very different way from how we deploy money or time. Expense decisions are sharply defined and very occasional; we typically only make a few per day. Decisions of how to spend our time are also fairly defined and are typically batched across just a handful of activities per day: nine hours working, half an hour for lunch, an hour for TV, half an hour to travel to and from work, and so on. Our minds, on the other hand, are churning every second. Sometimes our brains are focused on a task at hand, like executing a work project or having a conversation. But we spend significant portions of each day in relaxed, non-task-oriented thought, our minds wandering while we drive to and from work, eat lunch, walk to the bathroom, have dinner, and so on. Even when we are doing work that requires some level of concentration, we often have unrelated thoughts bubbling up on the peripheries of our attention.

This ongoing nonfocused cognitive processing can be a powerful resource. Steered in a certain direction, our nonfocused mental energy can lead to new insights, new ideas for businesses or programs, new strategies for improving efficiencies, and so on. It can also give us more energy, enthusiasm, and commitment to existing endeavors. All of this can be valuable for us personally and valuable for improving our ability to ease hardship in the world. Alternately, that mighty cognitive power can be expended on things that have comparatively little benefit to ourselves or others, such as self-centered reflections, rehashed conversations and arguments, idle replaying of content we absorbed from TV or social media, the latest sensationalized news headlines, and so on.

While we don't have complete control over the contents of our wandering minds, we do shape those contents with our choices of what to actively think about, what to care about, what to pay attention to, and how to spend our time. A theoretical physicist is going to have many more thoughts and ideas on physics unintentionally drifting into their mind while strolling through a park on Sunday than the average person. Someone who voluminously consumes cable news is going to find themselves inadvertently mulling over political issues much more often than the average person. If we find that our nonfocused thoughts consist primarily of useless trivialities or, even worse, that they consist of things that actively reduce our happiness or ability to achieve our goals in the world, we may want to reconsider what we are spending our time paying attention to and doing. We may also want to try being more attentive to the content of our nonfocused thoughts so we can nudge them in a more useful direction when needed.

Our nonfocused mental energy is not subject to the same zero-sum tug of war between benefiting ourselves and helping others that exists with our use of time and money. While we are generally quite intentional with how we use our money and time, most of the thoughts that pass through our wandering minds are not there because we consciously chose them; they are just the thoughts that happened to arise. Given we are not intentionally choosing them, it's not surprising that many of these thoughts are not particularly enjoyable; most are relatively neutral, and some can even be unenjoyable. What that means is we have a large amount of unfocused mental energy that can be redirected toward reducing the suffering of others without giving up anything we value. We don't have to forgo pleasurable uses of that mental energy to be able to put more of it toward helping those in need.

Let's turn now to our use of focused mental energy, where we intentionally put our cognitive power to use to understand a situation, solve a problem, or make a decision. We use this executive function of our brains all the time at work; an architect may spend an extensive amount of time thinking about, planning, drafting, and ultimately deciding on an exact design to use for a new high-rise office building. We also use this executive function all the time in our personal lives, from the smallest decisions (What should I buy for dinner?) to major ones (Should I buy a house? Should I encourage my parent to move into a nursing home?). Concentrated, deliberative thought is critical when making important work or personal decisions.

Similarly, when it comes to doing good, the amount of focused cognitive effort we put in can make an enormous difference for those who are suffering intensely. Consider again that the most effective charities can be ten thousand times more cost-effective at improving well-being than the majority of other charities. Given that huge disparity between organizations that at surface level may appear equally credible, putting in the mental work to make a carefully considered, data-driven decision on where to donate can mean the difference between improving the lives of hundreds of people in need and improving the life of just one. It can mean the difference between sparing hundreds of thousands of animals from a lifetime of cruelty and sparing just a few.

Unfortunately (in this regard), our brains were built to conserve energy, and so our instinct is typically to use the least amount of mental effort possible when making decisions that don't have major personal consequences. (Our bodies are similarly inclined to put in the least amount of physical effort possible, an inertia that must be overcome when starting a fitness regimen or beginning a daily workout.) That focus on conservation is one of the reasons we use heuristics to make snap judgments in lieu of more careful consideration—doing so helps us save mental energy. These mental shortcuts can have a major detrimental effect on the quality of our thinking and on the decisions we make when it comes to doing good in the world. Even though our choices in this area are incredibly consequential for many other individuals, and pertain to a cause we care deeply about, our brains will nevertheless prod us to minimize the amount of mental energy we spend thinking through them.

Consider, for example, the rules of thumb typically used when deciding whether to donate to a particular charity: Did we donate to that charity before? Do we like the leader personally? Did the stories they tell about their work strike an emotional chord with us? Are they working in a cause area we generally support? Do they have a decent reputation? If these boxes can be checked, we usually feel comfortable taking credit card in hand and making a gift. But the answers to these questions have vanishingly little correlation with how much good a charity will do with our donation. Considering and researching the answer to that key question requires a lot more cognitive effort (as well as more time) than we are naturally inclined to put into a donation decision. But just as getting physically fit requires overcoming our physical inertia, having a more significant positive impact in the world requires overcoming our cognitive inertia and putting in the mental work required.

That mental effort is needed not just when we're at the point of making a decision but also on a more day-to-day basis. Just as we need to regularly set aside time to exercise if we want to be more fit or to practice guitar if we want to be a better guitar player, if we want to be more effective at helping those in great need, we must regularly put in concentrated cognitive effort thinking through how to do that. That could involve taking time each week to research, read, and reflect on more effective ways to achieve our goal; investigating which programs and strategies appear to be particularly promising; periodically mulling on whether there are things other than giving to charity that might allow us to have a bigger impact; routinely considering how we can further optimize our use of time and money; and so on.

Unlike with unfocused mental energy, increasing the amount of intentional cognitive effort we put toward reducing misery in the world does come with a cost. Since our minds (and bodies) are geared toward conserving energy, putting in more effort quickly feels unpleasant and eventually feels downright painful. How long it takes before pleasurable or tolerable effort begins to feel unpleasant or painful depends on what we're used to, which in turn is a function of how much cognitive work we've done in the past. For experienced long-distance runners, a fifteen-mile jog could be enjoyable the entire time. For those who are very out of shape, a half mile jog could feel painful from the start. Similarly, for someone who is used to extended periods of mental focus (a scientist or academic for example), two hours of concentrated cognitive effort could be experienced as an enjoyable flow state. For someone else, spending even two minutes trying to understand a math equation or read a literary review journal could feel painful.

Putting in significantly more cognitive work to think through our uses of time and money and how we can better help those in need is no different. After a certain point, that additional mental effort will feel painful. Even the idea of putting in the work may generate a feeling of resistance. On top of that, thinking regularly about the hardships of others and the weighty consequences of our choices can be emotionally taxing, further adding to the mental load.

As a result, the personal trade-off we make when we increase the amount of focused mental energy we spend on helping those in need is the unpleasant feeling of cognitive strain. The zero-sum game we are often forced to play is choosing between cognitive comfort for ourselves and improved outcomes for those who are in need. This trade-off is not always present; much like the experienced long-distance runner or the mentally adroit academic, the more work we put in over time, the easier the work becomes. The increased mental effort can even become enjoyable for long stretches of time. There is, however, always some point of cognitive workload beyond which strain and discomfort begins and the zero-sum game re-emerges.

Strain or no strain, increasing our expenditure of mental energy is critical for doing good. Mental energy is the fuel that drives this work (and most work) forward. The more effort we put toward thinking through and understanding how to efficiently reduce the suffering of others, the more we will be able to achieve. Without the significant and ongoing cognitive work required to make smart decisions, it won't matter how generous we are with our money or time; those resources will partly or largely go to waste.

Carrying out that cognitive work requires both sustained diffuse mental energy as well as periodic focused mental energy. Keeping the plights of others and how we can better help them on constant simmer in the back of our minds, much like the ever-burning pilot light of a gas stove, will enable us to notice and act on many more opportunities for good. We will remember the potential impact of actions or inactions that previously would have seemed inconsequential. And we will know when to turn up the flame of focused mental energy to think through a situation more carefully and make a deliberate rather than an automatic choice. If we continually put both diffuse and focused mental energy to work, we will come to new insights and strategies that will enable us to make more effective decisions and more efficient use of our resources—doing a world of good for those in great need.

Perhaps reading this chapter has left you scratching your head. Is it reasonable or fair to view how much time we spend preparing lunch as an ethical question? When we're buying a pumpkin-spiced latte, do we really need to think about the malnourished children we could be feeding with that money instead? Do we really need to bear the emotional weight that comes from viewing every expenditure of time, money, and energy as an ethically consequential, decision?

It may seem overwhelming. It may seem unfair or unreasonable. It may seem just plain crazy.

As we have discussed, the reality of the world we live in presents us with what appears to be an ethically impossible standard. But when we strip away the ethereal notions relating to our own responsibility—our notions of what we should and shouldn't do, our judgments of whether we are good or bad—the simple reality of the world remains. And the reality of the world we live in today is that our mundane daily decisions can indeed have incredibly serious consequences for others. It is in fact the case that a latte, a lunch habit, and so on, these humdrum choices of action and inaction we make each day, can mean the difference between hunger and satiety, pain and relief, blindness and vision, misery and comfort, death and life, for many others with whom we share this world.

We may not like it, it may not be fair, and it may be overwhelming to think about. But what we think and feel about it doesn't change the fact that it is demonstrably true. It is a fact of modern life. So, what are you going to do?

CHAPTER SIX

Thinking Like an Athlete

*"If you choose to do something,
attack it...What put distance
between me and almost everybody
else in that platoon is that I
didn't let my desire for comfort
rule me. I was determined
to go to war with myself."*
—DAVID GOGGINS

Athletic Ethics

Looked at from one angle, this way of thinking and acting to reduce suffering in the world can seem mechanical, overly regimented, and unrealistically demanding. I would argue, though, that it's simply applying logic and rigor to the very common human sentiment of concern for others who are suffering. It's an approach squarely in line with Kierkegaard's admonition to consider our core beliefs, think them through to their logical conclusions, and act on those conclusions.

If taking an analytical and demanding approach to doing good for others seems odd, it is only because the altruism sector is often driven by emotion rather than logic and treated like a hobby rather than a serious endeavor. In other sectors, this mental and physical approach—where one rigorously optimizes and dedicates much of one's of time, energy, and resources toward achieving a central driving goal—is neither novel nor uncommon. The training and lifestyle required to be an elite performer in many prominent domains requires an equal or even greater level of regimentation, rigor, and sacrifice than what's advocated for in this book.

Consider, for example, professional athletes. Serious weightlifters and many professional fighters track their food intake obsessively, waking in the middle of each night to consume a carefully calibrated quantity of protein and supplements within a precise time window. Professional athletes have nearly their entire days regimented into rounds of practice, strength training, reviewing tapes of previous games, recovery periods, and so on—schedules dictated to them by coaches and managers. Other elite athletes, including those in certain Olympic sports, spend up to twelve hours a day in training for six to seven days each week, with nearly every element of their diets as well as their sleep and wake cycles tightly controlled. And all competitive athletes, along with their coaches, must continually think about what else they could be doing that they are not yet doing to further improve their game (their own version of the fourth box)—from diet tweaks to new workouts routines to new formations on the field.

Elite athletes aren't the only ones ordering their time, money, and energy in pursuit of a central goal. Consider the many millions of military enlistees past and present. Soldiers' lives are carefully optimized toward the goal of increasing their country's ability to dominate on the battlefield and thereby advance national interests. Active-duty soldiers spend years having their days regimented for them by commanding officers whose goal is to teach them relevant knowledge and skills, improve their ability to work as a unit, increase their physical fitness and their capacity to endure physical pain, and ready their willingness to kill and die. They are sent to and stationed at strategic outposts around the world for long periods of time, often separated from their families in the process. Most decisions on what they do, when they do it, and how they do it are made for them, and those decisions are not made based on what is best for the soldiers but on what best advances the military's central goal. And while in some countries military service is a requirement, there are millions of people who freely choose this way of life each year in countries such as the United States, United Kingdom, and others that do not have mandatory conscription.

This willingness to order so much of one's time, money, and energy toward a central goal can be found in other professions as well. Think, for example, of the up-front financial cost and the punishing work schedule required to become a medical doctor or the, perhaps, even more brutal work schedule of an investment banker. While their lives are less regimented in certain ways than those of athletes or soldiers—they can generally eat what they want when they want, they can choose which city to live in, and so on—the sheer number of work hours required necessitates serious sacrifice, including eliminating many of the activities and daily comforts most people take for granted. When workdays are sixteen to eighteen hours long or when work shifts are twenty-four hours in length, inadequate sleep, reduced time with family and friends, reduced health, and similar outcomes are not just sacrifices that surgeons or bankers can make to improve their performance, they are baseline prerequisites for even holding those jobs in the first place.

It's worth noting that the benefits of working to optimize one's life around a focal goal are particularly visible, and the use of such an approach particularly common, in domains where success is clearly measurable and reported on (such as marathon race times, the division between winners and losers in sports leagues, revenue generation for investment bankers, and so on) and when there are very strong personal incentives to succeed (such as large amounts of money, social stardom, or staying alive on a battlefield). The world of doing good for others largely lacks these incentivizing elements. While success can usually be measured, almost no one is measuring or comparing results between NGOs or other impact-focused entities, let alone between individuals at those entities or the funders financing them. Nor are there compelling financial incentives or social incentives to improve performance. This major difference in the incentive structure is probably a primary reason why so few people apply the same rigor, dedication, and self-sacrifice toward doing good for others that elite performers in other domains, such as professional athletes, routinely apply to theirs.

Naturally, we don't expect every physically active person to subject themselves to the level of effort that elite athletes put forth to reach and sustain high levels of performance. Most people don't have the desire or the ability to live that lifestyle. But those who do are generally looked at with admiration. Their self-discipline, work ethic, and singularity of focus on being the best they can be in their sport is viewed with great respect. Their level of effort is the grist for countless athletic apparel and sports drink commercials, and their example inspires amateur athletes, children, and aspiring pros to push harder in their own matches and training.

Similarly, while most people don't want a life in the armed forces, soldiers who take on the self-sacrifice of a regimented military life to contribute to what is generally considered a civic good are viewed with admiration and respect and as inspirational exemplars for doing more for one's country. Doctors are also accorded a great deal of respect and admiration, in part because they save lives but also because the public is aware of the level of mental and physical effort required to work in that profession. These are just a few examples; there are many other professions and sectors of society where carefully optimizing one's life around a central goal is viewed as not just sensible but also highly admirable.

Shouldn't we take the same view when it comes to efforts to reduce human and animal suffering? Such a goal is certainly a much more worthy cause to optimize one's life around than running faster or hitting a ball harder, and just as worthy as military service or saving lives in an operating room. Naturally, just as we wouldn't expect every casual gym-goer to put in the effort of an Olympian, we wouldn't expect every person who wants to make the world a better place to take the approach of an elite athlete, carefully structuring their time, money, and mental energy in a comprehensive regimen focused on helping those in need. But taking that approach to charity should be viewed as just as sensible as taking that approach to football, marathon running, military service, medicine, or similar endeavors. And as in those fields, it should be viewed as an admirable approach that can inspire others to push harder in their own similar endeavors.

In thinking about what it means to do all we can to make the world a better place, it would be useful to keep in mind a rule of thumb we'll call the Brady Rule. We could insert the name of nearly any highly successful athlete here, but legendary football quarterback Tom Brady's is a good one because of how well-known he is and because of his well-documented, hyper-focused approach toward optimizing his life and routines to reach and maintain peak levels of performance. In short, the Brady Rule is that if a certain approach worked for Tom Brady—if it helped him be a better football player—than a similar approach is likely helpful for being as effective as we can be at reducing suffering in the world.

If putting in a large number of hours helped Brady improve his performance, it would probably do the same for us. If carefully optimizing his life to remove distractions and concentrating just on football during the season helped Brady improve his performance, a similar approach would probably do the same for us. If carefully regimenting his diet to improve mental clarity and productivity helped Brady improve his performance, it would probably do the same for us. Again, that's not to say all of us should be expected to put in the same level of effort as a Tom Brady. He is a good model when it comes to work ethic and life optimization specifically because his approach was so exceptional. But the Brady Rule can be a useful reminder of what's required to perform at an exceptional level, whether we're playing football, working to alleviate pain and hardship in the world, or attempting to achieve anything else.

The comparison with the mental and physical approach used by elite performers in other domains also surfaces another important point. Addressing the fourth box is not simply a matter of doing a bunch of things we are not yet doing, the way we might check off items in a checklist. It's also a matter of cultivating a particular mindset. Rigorously optimizing our time, money, and energy around a central goal—be that improved athletic performance or reducing suffering—will not be possible in practice unless we develop in ourselves the mental attitudes and approaches necessary to successfully do so. These include fostering a strong internal drive to perform at the highest level we can, building our cognitive strength so we can direct our efforts in a more intelligent way and with greater mental stamina, accepting and even embracing discomfort as a prerequisite for growth, viewing personal sacrifice to benefit others as noble and often necessary as opposed to something to be avoided, dealing truthfully and practically with the trade-offs that exist in all of our decisions, and strengthening our self-discipline in order to see all of these things (and our work in general) through.

Let's look now at these additional mental attributes and the important role each plays in owning what we don't do and more effectively helping those who are suffering.

The Drive to Achieve

Why is it that elite performers are willing to put in so much effort and make real sacrifices to optimize their lives around a central goal?

The potential for large extrinsic personal rewards—like making a lot of money, earning social stardom, or keeping yourself and your friends alive on a battlefield—can obviously be very motivating. But clearly that's not everything. Many elite athletes, and many just below the elite level, know they will never make significant money or achieve public renown. And whether they are the world's fastest, twentieth fastest, or two hundredth fastest sprinter in a particular year has no effect on the lives of their family, friends or anyone else in the world. Yet, despite the seemingly trivial stakes, they are still willing to sacrifice so much and to structure their lives around advancing in their chosen endeavor. Why? What drives them?

In the field of psychology, the term used to describe a mind-set focused on achievement is "goal orientation." In everyday language, those who are driven to succeed and to achieve the most they are capable of achieving are sometimes referred to as being success-oriented. Whatever one calls it, this drive can be a profoundly powerful motivator on its own or in combination with other intrinsic or extrinsic motivations. And it's a drive that can fuel progress in whatever direction it's pointed, be that toward goals that have no meaningful impact on the world (for example running faster), goals that have a terrible impact (as far as murderous dictators go, Adolf Hitler was certainly one of the most ambitious and accomplished, by which of course we mean one of the worst), or goals that have a positive impact on the world.

When layered on top of altruistic concerns, a strong internal drive to achieve can be a powerful force for creating good outcomes in the world. It can be a much stronger motivator than extrinsic incentives like money or extrinsic disincentives like criticism. Interestingly, and human psychology being what it is, a strong internal drive to achieve can also be a more powerful motivator than the feelings of empathy or distress that come from thinking about those who are suffering. Seeing a photo or video of someone who is starving and thinking about what they are going through can be motivating. A strong internal drive to achieve, which leaves us regularly telling ourselves we can and should be doing a better job than we are now of helping those who are starving, can be even more motivating.

Another way to say this is that focusing on ourselves in a particular way—namely, focusing on our performance and our potential—can lead us to be more successful at reducing the suffering of others than focusing on those who are suffering. This sounds counterintuitive, but it makes sense when we consider that the only way to achieve more change for others is by changing and improving the tool that is our self: becoming more thoughtful, hard-working, persuasive, giving, and so on.

Being success-oriented is probably not a simple singular drive but rather some combination of psychological predispositions. These might include heightened feelings of guilt, duty, egotism, insecurity, or dissatisfaction; heightened levels of obsessive tendencies, novelty-seeking, or competitiveness; or other things entirely. The exact combination certainly varies person to person, both for elite athletes and for those who want to make the world a better place.

Regardless of the specific contributing factors, a strong drive to achieve the most we can is a powerful force. And like so many internal dispositions, while the strength of that drive is shaped in part by genetics, we can also influence it with our beliefs and choices.

Internally, we can acknowledge and appreciate the value that ambition and a success-orientation have for creating positive change for others. We can choose to set higher standards for our work and loftier expectations of what we believe we should be able to achieve. And we can fan the flames of whatever elements in us contribute to our own internal drive to achieve all that we can.

Externally, the strength of our drive to achieve will be influenced by our environment, and most of us have at least a modest amount of control over which work, social and cultural environments we choose to enmesh ourselves in. Consider for example the cultural elements we choose to surround ourselves with: the social media channels we follow, the podcasts and news stations we listen to, the magazines and blogs we read, the people we choose to talk to regularly, and so on. We humans are a highly memetic species, and the voices, attitudes, and concerns of those we choose to pay attention to will have a major influence on our own approach to life in every area—including how dedicated and driven we are to do all we can for those in extreme suffering.

For those of us who work at or are involved with NGOs, we should also consider the Brady Rule in reflecting on what sort of culture we would like to have around us to be able to perform at the highest level we can. For example, if an organizational culture that was intently focused on winning and that made decisions accordingly helped Brady and his team as a whole improve their performance, it would probably do the same for us and ours. If having coaches and trainers set high expectations and standards and give challenging feedback when it was warranted helped Brady give his all, it would probably do the same for us. If having teammates who expected and celebrated extra effort and sacrifice from one another (and themselves) helped Brady perform at his best, it would probably do the same for us.

Building Cognitive Strength and Stamina

If our goal is to own what we don't do, to identify the good things we are not yet doing but could be doing and carry them out, as noted earlier money and time are only useful if we know how to use them well. The domain-specific intelligence and ability we develop to make smart, creative, and effective decisions will have a major impact on how far our limited time and money can go to help those in extreme suffering. And that means that how well we develop our overall cognitive strength and abilities—our mental stamina, self-discipline, processing speed, and general mental sharpness—will have a major effect on how much we're able to achieve for others. Just as athletes can build up their physical strength, so too can we build up these cognitive strengths in ourselves.

Physical and cognitive capabilities are partly genetically predetermined. They are also unequally distributed, with different people having different levels of potential. But both are also meaningfully influenced by environment and personal choice. Elite athletes who win gold medals and league championships aren't able to do so simply because they won the genetic lottery in areas like height or fast-twitch muscle-fiber mass, nor are scientists who win the Nobel Prize able to do so simply because they were born with a high IQ. Genetic gifts certainly lift the ceiling on what's possible, but getting anywhere close to that physical or cognitive ceiling—and for us getting anywhere close to our own personal potential—requires hard work done consistently over a long period of time. This includes both direct work as well as working to create the right environmental conditions for ourselves.

WHAT WE DON'T DO

Consider the physical speed and endurance of twin sisters who are born with nearly identical genes and experience nearly identical early environments. One sister wakes up most mornings to run for one to two hours, pushing herself to improve her speed on many of those runs. She sticks with this regimen for years, while also spending time learning about and carefully following a nutritionally excellent diet. The second sister doesn't run at all or do much other exercise, and she eats a relatively unhealthy diet. As a result, the first sister can run a marathon in four hours and feel fine the next day, while the second sister is not able to run even a quarter of a mile without stopping to catch her breath. This vast difference in capability is purely a function of difference of effort—how hard each sister worked physically for how long a period of time, and how much mental rigor and self-discipline each brought to bear in the process.

The range of potential for our own cognitive abilities is just as wide as the difference between the breezing marathoner and the breathless quarter-miler. And where we stand on that range is just as much a direct function of the amount of effort we put in and the self-discipline we bring to bear to do so. Whatever package of genetics we happened to be born with, just as we can build up our physical strength and stamina so too can we increase our cognitive strength (our overall intelligence, shrewdness of judgment, ability to identify patterns, ability to eliminate bias, and so on) and our cognitive stamina (our ability to stick with a challenging project for a longer period of time, to manage multiple mental work streams effectively, and so forth). Since overall cognitive ability—from good judgment and clear thinking to creativity and processing speed—is a critical factor in how successful we will be at helping those in need, the level of effort we put into building up that ability is also critical.

With physical exercise, the only way to get larger muscles is by pushing those muscles until they literally break in the form of microtears. It is these microtears that stimulate new muscle tissue to develop, allowing overall muscle mass to increase. The only way to lift a heavier weight comfortably is to lift that weight uncomfortably many times first. The only way to run a faster mile breathing normally is to run a faster mile panting many times first. Soreness is progress. Discomfort is progress. As the expression goes, no pain no gain.

Similarly, growing in cognitive capability requires being continually dissatisfied with where we are at now, with our current level of understanding, abilities and output. It requires continually pushing ourselves outside of our comfort zone, asking what we are missing or what we have gotten wrong up until now. It requires routinely challenging ourselves to work longer, harder, faster, and in different and more efficient ways.

Like with physical exercise, putting in that effort can feel unpleasant. As a result, our inclination can be to settle into cognitive routines that limit our mental effort to a comfortably low level. This is visible across all professions and areas of life, including among those who donate, volunteer or work with NGOs. Externally this can look like giving to the same places, carrying out the same programs, focusing on the same chartable sub-sectors, doing work at the same pace, and so on. Cognitively this can look like maintaining a static level of effort or gradually declining that effort over time, contentment with the current level of results, and continuing to think about and approach social problems in the same way. It's the cognitive equivalent of a casual jogger who puts in a few miles on the treadmill at a comfortable pace twice a week.

Have we experienced cognitive pain this week by pushing our mental energy past the realm of what's comfortable and into the realm of being overtaxed, tired, wanting to quit? It is this soreness that builds cognitive endurance and our ability to pull more productivity out of our limited time and our limited days. Have we made metaphorical micro-tears in our current ways of thinking and working over the past few months? It is the continual questioning of current approaches and testing of new and unfamiliar approaches that enables us to discover more efficient ways of getting things done.

It's worth noting that what we feed our bodies and, consequently, our brains also plays an important role. Those rigorously working to build bigger muscles don't just lift progressively heavier weights to cause micro-tears. They also increase their intake of protein and branched-chain amino acids and creatine, since doing so leads to faster muscle recovery and growth; avoid eating unhealthy foods; try to get sufficient sleep; and so on. All these things, when coupled with the regular strain of lifting progressively heavier weights, contribute to improved results.

We can and should put in the same research, testing, and planning around the inputs and other factors that affect our cognitive strength and stamina. This can include consuming the right levels of caffeine and glucose (there is abundant research on the effect each of these has for improving mental performance); getting adequate sleep (there is also abundant research on its importance for mental sharpness and productivity); engaging in regular physical exercise; eating healthy, including consuming more of the vegetables, nuts, and spices that appear to be linked to increased cognitive performance; and working with rather than against the natural fluctuations in energy our bodies have over the course of a day. Much like with physical body building, none of this is a replacement for regularly putting in the unpleasant strain of hard cognitive work. But coupled with that work, it can lead to significantly better results: more mental strength and stamina, and the fruits those things can bear.

Much like with physical effort, pushing our cognitive capacity beyond its comfort zone is neither easy nor enjoyable. It requires exercising self-discipline and accepting the unpleasant feeling of mental strain on a daily and ongoing basis. But there is simply no way to get to the level of productivity and the level of impact we are capable of without that effort and that strain, just as there is no way for an elite athlete to get to the level of performance they are capable of without similar physical effort and strain.

And that brings us to another critical mental element for owning the fourth box: accepting and even embracing discomfort.

Embracing Discomfort

A willingness to bear discomfort is part and parcel of a strong work ethic, and it is a critical factor in the success of most elite athletes. Those who arrive to practice early, push themselves harder during it, and stay late to challenge themselves for longer are the ones more likely to advance to higher levels of performance. Is there any athlete who has achieved a significant level of skill without putting themselves through routine discomfort and times of outright suffering?

It's a truism in fitness communities that the days you really don't want to go for a run or really don't want to walk into a gym are the days it's most important to do so. That ethos is partly a commentary on the importance of habit and self-discipline, but it is also about cultivating a mindset of embracing discomfort. Since strain and discomfort are critical for growth, and since our natural inclination is to avoid those things, having an attitude of actively embracing discomfort is key. The choice of whether or not to embrace discomfort, and of how much we are willing to take on, will strongly influence how far we can go in any endeavor.

While we focused in the previous section on putting in the mental effort and taking on the mental strain necessary to build cognitive strength, a similar principle applies to our use of time and money. Beyond a certain limited amount, giving more of our time or more of our money can feel quite unpleasant. But just as the more we push ourselves physically and mentally the more we can comfortably tolerate physical and mental effort, the more we give of our time and money the more we can comfortably tolerate such giving. Contributing our money and time to a level that causes discomfort is what will generate the metaphorical micro-tears of our charity muscle, building its strength and allowing us to comfortably give similar or greater amounts in the future.

When we really don't want to give more of our money or time or mental energy, when we know it's not going to feel good and yet we push forward and do it anyway, those are the times we know we're increasing our own capabilities for making the world a better place. If we don't feel discomfort from what we're doing now, how are we going to be able to do more in the future? Once again: no pain, no gain.

Unfortunately, this is not the mindset with which charitable work is typically approached. The expectation most have is that charitable work should be a feel-good endeavor, one that is carried out in a way that makes the doer feel good. To ask a set of rhetorical questions: How many staffers at nonprofit organizations do you think show up for work in the morning with the mindset of an elite athlete on a training regimen, ready and eager to embrace discomfort because that is the path to improved performance? How many donors to charitable causes do you think approach their philanthropy with the mindset of a soldier at boot camp, ready to "embrace the suck" (to borrow a term from the Marines) in the name of a cause they believe in? Among those who say one of their key goals in life is to make the world a better place, how many have developed a challengingly rigorous routine structured toward achieving that goal?

These questions are rhetorical because the answer to each is obvious: not many. Why is that the case? After all, many people do care deeply about certain charitable causes. And we know there are tens of millions of professional athletes, soldiers, surgeons, investment bankers, and others who are willing to do these things and more to succeed in their own professions.

Is it merely, as mentioned earlier, the lack of sufficiently compelling personal incentives in the realm of charity and philanthropy, given impact is rarely quantified and potential personal gains and losses are limited? Is it due in part to differences in personality, with those who are drawn to charitable sectors often having personality types that differ from those drawn to elite athletics, the military, highly demanding white-collar occupations, and similar careers? Is it due to differences in the prevailing organizational cultures in each sector, differences which have reinforced themselves and grown larger over time?

Attempting to answer such questions would be beyond the scope of this book. And the goal here is not to issue blanket criticism of a sector made up of many different people with different personalities and highly varying levels of effort. Rather, the goal is to encourage those of us who want to reduce suffering in the world to reflect on what personal examples we look to for reference and inspiration—and whose standards we hold ourselves to when it comes to effort, sacrifice, and mindset. Do we hold ourselves to the standards of elite athletes, who have much to gain? Do we hold ourselves to the standards of active-duty soldiers, who have much to lose? Or are the role models we look to far different and the standards far lower?

Another way to think about this would be to ask ourselves the following questions: What are we willing to do to be more successful at achieving our goals? What are we willing to do to achieve more progress for the causes we claim to care deeply about? Are we willing to put the same level of focus, rigor, and effort toward a goal like reducing the extreme suffering of others that hundreds of thousands of others around the world are right now putting toward the goal of running faster, jumping farther, or lifting heavier objects? Are we willing to embrace the same discomfort and trade-offs that a professional athlete embraces to help their team win and their career advance? Are we willing to sacrifice the same comforts and conveniences that millions of soldiers sacrifice for both personal and civic-minded goals? Are we willing to take on the same number of work hours that hundreds of thousands of investment bankers, surgeons, and others take on to succeed and earn a great deal of money in their professions?

Whatever we think of athletes, soldiers, surgeons, investment bankers, and so on—whether we think their use of time and energy is sensible or not, whether we think their occupation is a good use of a life or not, whether we think their professions should or shouldn't operate the way they do—is largely irrelevant. The point is simply that many other people in the world are willing to embrace a very significant amount of discomfort, put in a very significant amount of effort, and accept a very significant level of regimentation and optimization of their lives in order to achieve goals that are no more important and often far less important than reducing extreme suffering in the world. If millions of others are willing to do so for their goals, and are doing so right now, then certainly we can do the same. The question is, are we willing to? If not, why? Do we really want to put less rigor and effort into ending the extreme misery of tens of thousands of others than Tom Brady put into throwing a football more accurately?

Sacrifice

Periodically giving up physically and mentally comfortable states to endure and even embrace discomfort in the name of progress is a type of sacrifice. But for most who have achieved great success, the sacrifices they made didn't end there. Most needed to make other sacrifices as well, forgoing things they would have liked to have done or to have had so they could achieve their goal. This may have meant sacrificing leisure time, sleep, or personal hobbies. It may have meant earning less money, missing hangouts with family and friends, or passing on other personal or career opportunities. What was sacrificed may have been something still greater. Given achieving higher levels of success in one area almost always requires intentional sacrifices in other areas, it's worth taking some time to consider the nature of sacrifice and its importance for addressing the fourth box.

It should be noted outright that there is nothing noble about sacrifice for its own sake. Like a medieval monk flagellating himself with a cat-o'-nine-tails, mini martyrdoms of our time, money, energy, health or happiness that produce no equivalent or larger good in the world are at best an unfortunate waste of those valuable things. This type of self-sacrifice is often ultimately self-focused, driven by a desire for personal purity, meaning, self-expression, or some other internal outcome—or occasionally by a mental health issue. At other times, fruitless self-sacrifice may simply be the result of a well-intentioned but naïve effort by someone who is new to a particular cause area or who has not been exposed to more practical models for creating change.

On the other hand, calculated sacrifice—where we make the choice to give up some happiness or endure some hardship so that others can experience real, demonstrable benefit—is a decision that is both noble and commonplace. Putting others' interests before our own is something humans have done for hundreds of thousands of years. Tribe members sacrificing their lives to protect fellow tribe members from an attacking animal, parents working in sweatshops so they can afford to send their children to school, and firefighters running into a burning building to save the lives of those trapped inside are examples that just scratch the surface of the calculated sacrifices humans have made throughout history and across cultures. Sometimes these sacrifices are one-time events in extraordinary circumstances, and sometimes they are a choice made daily. Sometimes they are made for the sake of friends and family members, and other times they are made for complete strangers.

Just what is it that we are sacrificing when we direct significantly more of our money, time, and energy to those in need?

Quite simply, we are sacrificing anything those resources could have brought us. When it comes to money, we are forgoing anything we would have otherwise purchased with that money: any object, experience, status, gift, and so on. When it comes to time, we are sacrificing whatever we would have otherwise done with that time: any event, experience, social gathering, hobby, or so on. And when it comes to mental energy, while certainly there are specific pleasurable (or neutral) uses of mental energy we may sacrifice to undertake the cognitive effort of regularly thinking through how to make the world a better place, perhaps the biggest sacrifice we make in this area is taking on the emotional weight of thinking regularly about others' suffering and feeling responsible for doing what we can to help them.

If we feel ourselves chafing at the idea of working overtime or forgoing eating out to be able to donate more money to effective charities, or if the notion of spending several hours each week thinking through how we can better help those in misery seems too emotionally or cognitively demanding, reflecting on the sacrifices made by millions of people in other areas of life can provide some helpful perspective. Consider the millions of soldiers in and around active combat zones who are putting their own lives at risk (whether for good or for ill); the tens of millions of parents around the world who have left their homes and everything they know to immigrate to a safer and richer country so that their children might be able to have a better life; the police officers running onto the scene of an active shooter situation; and so on.

Addressing the fourth box, owning what we don't do, doesn't require putting our life on the line, even though many around the world are doing exactly that to protect others. It doesn't require risking our health and safety or enduring degrading and brutal conditions, even though many around the world are choosing to endure those things so that others may benefit. Addressing the fourth box simply calls for a regular giving of our time, money, and mental energy. And if many around the world are willing to sacrifice so much, shouldn't we be willing to give those things to the point of sacrificing some real amount of our own happiness and comfort to help those in extreme suffering?

These rhetorical questions beg a more practical question: Just how much should we give to those in need? Just how much should we sacrifice? Earlier we discussed how the zero-sum reality of the world we live in is that every dollar or hour we use for our own benefit is a dollar or hour not used to benefit someone suffering in extreme misery. At first blush, the logic of this book might therefore seem to suggest acting ethically requires sacrificing everything—giving away every penny of our money and every minute of our time (and every ounce of our mental energy to boot). But to answer this question more thoughtfully, it's instructive to consider once again the lifestyle of an elite athlete.

Although encouragements to "leave everything on the field" and "give it everything you've got" are popular in sports, no professional athlete truly gives everything they have, at least not in the short term. Elite athletes push themselves hard. But an athlete who pushed their body past a certain point would experience a debilitating physical breakdown that prevented them from continuing to perform well. For example, training to be an elite marathoner requires running a lot of training miles, way past the point of enjoyment or comfort. But the correlation between miles run and improvement in performance is not linear. Beyond a certain point, running additional training miles becomes harmful to achieving top performance. Those who continue running past that point will experience a decline in performance. Those who keep running further still will eventually collapse in exhaustion and end up in the hospital, unable to even walk—let alone win a marathon.

Similarly, while giving away all the money we had today might do some good and might make some people feel a sort of spiritual piety, it would not be the most effective way to help those in need. For one thing, we'd have no resources left to do additional good with in the future. Secondly, because over time we should be able to discover more cost-efficient ways of doing good, assuming we both put in the mental effort and follow through with eventually giving, we may be able to do several times or even tens or hundreds of times more good with each dollar we donate several years in the future than we can do with each dollar we donate now. Lastly, if we did give away truly everything and had no financial resources left for ourselves, we would have to spend significant amounts of our time looking after our own survival instead of being able to use that time to help others.

Practically speaking, of course all of us want to and are going to seek some amount of happiness, pleasure, and comfort in our lives, some of which requires money to procure. But even if we were to hypothetically operate from a place of complete altruism, with no concern whatsoever for personal happiness for its own sake, we'd need to use some portion of our money, time and mental energy to benefit ourselves if we wanted to achieve our altruistic goal. Without some minimal level of mental health and happiness, and of physical health and comfort, we would eventually become the psychological or physical replica of the marathoner who simply doesn't stop running. Our brains and bodies would begin to break down, and we'd be unable to do much (or as much as we could) to help those in need.

An athlete who pushed their body to the point at which it broke down into clinical exhaustion, or a person who literally gave their last dollar to charity or who gave all of their time and mental energy to the point of experiencing severe mental misery, would not be someone able to perform at their peak. They would not be following the path that enabled them to best achieve their goal. At best they would be acting thoughtlessly, and more likely they would be operating under the influence of some dysfunctional psychological mechanism.

In the charity sector as in other sectors, the term "burnout" is often used to refer to the scenario in which someone who had been highly engaged with their work experiences such a sharp drop in motivation that they find it difficult to continue. Sometimes this is the result of doing too much, as the sheer number of hours worked leads to sleep deprivation, inadequate nutrition and exhaustion. In many other cases burnout is less a function of volume and more a function of process: how a person mentally and emotionally engages with their work, how calm or stressful their relationships are with peers, and to what level they feel things like autonomy, mastery and purpose.

Endeavoring to help those in need can significantly turn up the dials on emotions such as distress, powerlessness, urgency, anger and guilt, which over time can lead to the feeling of burnout as well. The cratering of motivation that can result from this is common enough to have birthed related terms such as "compassion fatigue" and "donor fatigue." (In my own experience working in the charity and philanthropy sectors for two decades, I've seen many people experience burnout from the way they emotionally engage with their work or for other process-related reasons; only a few experience burnout from working too many hours; and none experience burnout or other personal downsides from giving away too much money.)

While the causes of burnout are often more complex and the warning signs more subtle than they are in the case of athletes who push their bodies too hard, the Brady Rule remains a useful guiding principle for those working to help others. We should push ourselves to expand our limits—accepting and even embracing the feeling of strain that comes with doing so—while staying attuned to what those limits are and not pushing recklessly past them. While it's outside the scope of this book to cover properly, there are a wide range of techniques that others use to be able to do and produce more while remaining happy, healthy and enjoyably engaged with their work. Examples include healthy eating, exercise, good sleep, moderate levels of caffeine, meditation, cultivating hobbies and social ties unrelated to work, personal organization and time management improvements, and developing healthier ways of thinking about and emotionally engaging with their work. There are countless how-to books and articles on these tools, and each of us can learn about and draw on them in whatever ways work best for our own particular psychology and situation.

That said, the reality is very few of us are anywhere close to the point of spending so much time or giving so much money or mental energy to help others that we are actually harming our ability to do good. Nearly every one of us could go significantly further in the direction of shifting more time, money, and energy toward helping those in extreme misery while still remaining adequately healthy and happy. Nearly every one of us is on the side of "could be doing more," not the side of "should be doing less." The gap between what we're doing now and what we could be doing, while still staying adequately healthy and happy, is our own fourth box.

The term "adequately" is used quite intentionally here. It is not the case that the happier we are the more we will be able to do for others, and that the less happy we are, the less we will be able to do for others. It is only for those rare cases where someone's unhappiness is so pronounced it is meaningfully eroding their work that increasing their happiness would allow them to do more for others. There are often real trade-offs we must make between increasing our own short-term happiness and doing more to reduce the suffering of others, just as there are trade-offs between short-term enjoyment and achieving higher levels of success in any domain.

Doing progressively more to help those in need will often result in small decreases in our own comfort and enjoyment. The place of peak performance is not the most comfortable place for our bodies or minds. It is usually a place where we are undergoing real mental or physical strain and real loss of pleasure (at least for periods of time)—but not so much as to cause a destructive breakdown or a drop in total output. That is the sacrifice those who wish to be top performers in any domain must make. Without it, the ceiling on what can be achieved drops considerably.

CHAPTER SEVEN
Dealing Honestly
with Trade-offs

*"Every step toward the goal of
justice requires sacrifice."*
—MARTIN LUTHER KING, JR.

Personal Trade-offs

When we talk about sacrifice, we are talking about trade-offs. Trade-offs can be between competing personal goods or goals, where we accept less of one thing we want so we can have more of another thing we want. If we like going to Broadway shows but also like going to the beach and only have the money and time to do one of those this weekend, we might pass on the theater in order to have a day at the shore. Trade-offs can also be between goods for ourselves and goods for others, where we benefit and others lose or where others benefit and we lose. For example, we may be choosing between putting an extra $2,000 into a savings account for ourselves and donating that money to help those in need. (We could also view this as a trade-off between competing personal goals, namely between a big-picture preference we have for less suffering in the world and a personal preference we have for the comfort of increased financial security.)

If we want to own our inactions and do the most good we can in the world, we need to be honest about the fact that we are almost always making trade-offs in one direction or another.

For example, as we were just noting, the place of peak performance is not usually the most comfortable place for our minds and bodies; it's usually a place where we are undergoing real strain and some temporary loss of pleasure, although not so much as to cause a destructive breakdown. As one element of this, let's look at the relationship between number of hours worked and productivity—a relationship that ultimately leads to the trade-off between enjoyment for ourselves and benefits for others.

Most of us (though certainly not all) enjoy working to some extent. We would not be happy doing nothing all day, and a moderate amount of work feels enjoyable or, at least, relatively neutral. That said, there is always some line beyond which work starts to feel unenjoyable. All other things being equal, we'd rather stop working at that point and do something else. The work we do beyond that point is a trade-off between our personal enjoyment in the short term and something else we want in the longer term. We trudge through more work now so we can pay the rent, go to the movies, or take a vacation in the future. Or, if we are addressing the fourth box, we trudge through more work so we can have more money to help those in great need, or to do more for them directly. The point at which work starts to be unenjoyable is the point at which we face a trade-off between personal enjoyment and productivity.

In recent decades, the idea has sometimes been put forth that a trade-off between enjoyment and productivity is either nonexistent or is far more minimal than we may have thought. The basic premise of the argument is that beyond a certain number of hours, our productivity begins to decline. The number of hours that is often claimed to be ideal for peak productivity is usually a number modestly lower than whatever the local norm happens to be. When the argument is made in European countries with a thirty-five to forty-hour average work week, the number of hours that allows for peak productivity is often claimed to be twenty to thirty-five hours. In the United States, where a standard work week is forty to forty-five hours, the number is often claimed to be thirty to thirty-five hours or a four-day (thirty-two-hour) work week. As a result, the argument states, we can work fewer hours than we do now—something most of us would find very enjoyable—with no loss of productivity and, perhaps, even some productivity gains.

While the idea sounds great in theory, unfortunately it is simply not true. Or to be more precise, it is rarely true; it is true only if we currently work an extremely high number of hours.

The most frequently cited research paper on the topic is "The Productivity of Working Hours" by Stanford researcher John Pencavel. Pencavel's study looked at the work hours and productivity of manual laborers (mostly female) in a munitions factory during World War I. The study found that a person's hourly productivity did not begin to decline until they moved above fifty hours of work per week. Even as they move beyond that level into work weeks of fifty-five to sixty hours and above, total weekly (or overall) productivity continued to increase.

The gradual waning of hourly productivity beyond the fifty-hour mark was more than compensated for by the increased total number of hours worked. It was only when workers got to a significantly higher number of hours per week—between the low sixties to seventy hours per week—that total weekly productivity began to drop. As a result, those who worked seventy hours per week were no more productive than those who worked fifty-five hours per week. The number of weekly work hours that led to the highest overall productivity seemed to sit in the low sixties. (It's worth keeping in mind that this is the average across all workers and there was likely individual variation; presumably, some were more productive at seventy hours and some more productive at fifty-five hours. It's also worth keeping in mind that the work in question was physically demanding labor in a munitions factory.)

Other studies on the interplay between work hours and productivity, including studies of white-collar workers and call-center workers, have generally found similar results: after a certain number of hours per week, hourly productivity began to gradually decline but overall productivity continued to increase. Only when work weeks reached some number of hours very significantly above forty hours per week did overall productivity began to decline. The studies also found that the eventual declines in hourly productivity only occurred for workers who were required to work a larger number of hours. For those who voluntarily chose to work additional hours, there was no decline in hourly productivity (at least not within the range of hours covered by the study).

Upon reflection, this should also not come as a real surprise. How many highly successful and fast-growing businesses were built by founders who worked only thirty to forty hours a week? How would greatest-of-all-time NFL quarterback Tom Brady's career have turned out if he emphasized to coaches that work-life balance was important to him and he was not willing to put in more than forty hours a week?

It's important to note here that none of this is a commentary on how many hours per week any specific person should work, or on how many hours an employer should want or expect their staffers to work. Those are very different questions and, therefore, can have different answers. For example, the research suggests that companies running call centers and that pay staffers on an hourly basis may well want to limit shifts to five or six hours per day to achieve the most productivity per dollar of staff cost. Similarly, to not miss out on talented candidates, it might make sense for employers to expect and require only the number of work hours that is standard in their region—typically forty to forty-five hours per week. And on the individual level, for those whose primary goal is to enjoy life more it may well make sense to work twenty hours a week or less. (The wildly popular book *The 4-Hour Workweek* is the result of author Timothy Ferris' experiments in how he could live a comfortable and enjoyable life while putting in the minimum number of work hours possible.)

But what the existing literature on work hours and productivity makes clear is that for those who want to achieve more with their work—to make more money, to make more widgets, or to make the world a better place—but who don't personally enjoy working sixty-five hours a week or longer, the trade-off between overall productivity and personal enjoyment is real. Benefits in one area come at the expense of something or someone else. If our goal is to use our time to help reduce extreme suffering in the world, and we cut off our efforts at forty hours per week to have a more enjoyable work-life balance, we are leaving a huge amount of potential good we can do on the table. Here as in most situations, trade-offs exist. We are almost always choosing between competing goods.

The idea that we can work fewer hours while still being just as productive is akin to the more general notion from the charitable sector that the happier we are, the more effective we'll be (and the more good we'll be able to do do for others), and that the less happy we are, the less effective we'll be. That notion seems to stem from an intuition that what is better for us will generally also be better (or at least not harmful) for others. A good outcome for us and a good outcome for others goes hand in hand in linear correlation. This tendency to believe that trade-offs don't exist or can be avoided is quite pronounced in the charity sector.

For example, philanthropic donors are often encouraged—including by professional charitable giving advisors—to support the causes they are most passionate about. The theory behind this advice is that it creates a win-win situation: the donor feels very good about giving and remains engaged over time, while the recipient charity gets a nice gift with which they can do good work. Unfortunately, there's a trade-off to the good feeling a donor gets by giving to the cause they're most passionate about. When a donor picks a charity based on personal passion, their gift will almost surely do far less good—likely several orders of magnitude less good—than when they pick a charity based on how cost-effective that charity is at reducing suffering or increasing well-being. To pick a charity based on personal passion is therefore to prioritize one's own enjoyment in giving the gift over achieving the maximum amount of good in the world. It is to choose one's own happiness over others' suffering in a real and consequential way.

This may sound harsh and unappreciative of those who are doing the giving. Shouldn't critique be directed at those who are not giving at all, as opposed to those who are trying to do something good even if they may not be choosing the most effective charity? Perhaps. But the point here is that trade-offs exist in philanthropy just as they do in most areas of life. Charitable giving is rarely a win-win scenario where the warm glow of donating goes perfectly hand-in-hand with the amount of good done for the world. In most cases, donors must choose between the competing goods of getting more enjoyment for themselves from the act of giving and reducing substantially more suffering in the world.

For those working in the charity sector, we can see the same tension if we return to our discussion on work hours and the concept that the happier employees are—thanks to shorter work hours, but also higher salaries, control over what they work on, work hours, opportunities for growth, how nurturing their managers are, how close they are to other staffers, and so on—the more productive they will be and the more good work will be done. This notion has a common-sense ring to it, and it is certainly appealing because it suggests there are no trade-offs that need to be wrestled with. Making work conditions more enjoyable is a win-win situation.

But like most notions that deny the presence of trade-offs, this one is demonstrably not true. Or to be more precise, this will only be true when the current work environment is particularly miserable, or when staffers are working eighty or ninety hour weeks, just as running fewer training miles would only be helpful for a marathoner who is running an excessive number of miles. As is the case with marathon training and work weeks, the relationship between employee happiness and employee productivity is a nonlinear relationship. Achieving maximal staff happiness might entail two-hour workdays, free daily massages, opulent free food and beverages, exorbitantly high salaries, and the ability to work on whatever one wanted to work on—all of which would clearly generate a crash in productivity.

While the things that make a workplace more enjoyable can certainly have some relationship with productivity, the relationship is a nonlinear one. At certain points on the continuum of a completely miserable to phenomenally comfortable workplace, we really can have our cake and eat it too, with increases in individual enjoyment going hand in hand with increases in productivity. But at most points in the continuum, these two goods stand in active competition with one another. The relationship between shorter work hours and overall productivity is one area where we have meaningful data showing when and how these goods stand in competition. Similar trade-offs exist for nearly every factor that makes for a more enjoyable workplace. Too much creative autonomy, too high salaries, and overall company productivity almost surely goes down. There is a reason we have the phrase "too much of a good thing"—the benefit of good things is never ceaselessly linear.

Whenever something that makes a workplace more enjoyable for employees comes into conflict with overall productivity, we are faced with a trade-off. Choices must be made about which good to prioritize. It may be difficult for decisionmakers in these scenarios to accept or impartially weigh the competing goods. One set of recipients of those goods—a charity's employees—are the people the decisionmaker sees and speaks to and works with every day, and may also be friends with. Those recipients will think better or worse of the decisionmaker based on their decision. The other set of recipients—those in need whom the charity is working to help—are often out of sight, are rarely friends with the decisionmaker, and in any case will not treat the decisionmaker better or worse based on their decision. In the absence of some countervailing force, the personal incentive for decisionmakers will often be to prioritize small goods to their staff over major goods to those their charity is aiming to help. They are more likely to receive some small but real personal benefit, including feeling better about themselves, when they make trade-offs in that direction. That said, people and workplaces of course differ dramatically, and there are certainly charities where improvements in employee happiness in certain areas would likely improve productivity.

The key point is that with any decision we make, we are almost always choosing between competing goods. Choosing in favor of one usually requires choosing at the expense of another. Accepting and dealing honestly with the reality of trade-offs is critical if we want to own the fourth box and do the most good we can for others. Once we do accept that trade-offs exist, the ongoing challenge we are faced with is noticing what the trade-offs are in any given situation and accurately weighting the competing goods that are at stake.

For most of human history, harms came primarily from the natural world in the form of famine, disease, drought, natural disasters, animal attacks, and so on and secondarily from direct violent conflict with other human beings in the form of physical attacks and war. These sorts of threats certainly remain today, but they are no longer the driving force of human misery. Today, much if not most of that pantheon of suffering is the consequence of individuals, companies, and governments choosing to view trivial benefits to themselves (and their families, constituents and allies) as more important than very major harms endured by others.

Examples of this are nearly endless. Consider the treatment of workers in sweatshops, where slightly lower prices for wealthy consumers are judged to be a more important outcome than the dramatically less-cruel conditions for workers that could be achieved with slightly higher prices (assuming the marginal difference in price was used to improve conditions at factories). Or consider our treatment of the environment, where the benefit of trivial conveniences such as plastic bags and bottled water are viewed as more important than the downsides they create such as pollution, carbon emissions, waste, and the killing of wildlife.

Or consider the treatment of animals on factory farms, where slightly lower prices for customers—including in the world's wealthiest nations—are judged as more important than animals having relief from the cruelest intensive confinement systems. In a flagrant example of this, many mother pigs—who are more intelligent than dogs—are confined for nearly their entire four-year lives in barren metal crates so small they cannot turn around. Switching to alternative systems that allow mother pigs to walk around, lie down comfortably, and so on increases the production cost of pork by a mere 1 percent—equivalent to two to three cents per pound in wealthy western countries. Yet, it has taken decades of work by advocates to persuade just some companies and governments to make that change.

It's understandable that any person, company, or government would weight goods and harms to themselves as more important than goods and harms to others. The problem is that when goods and harms to others happen out of sight, we often don't assign them any weight whatsoever. Typically, we don't even think about them. And today, almost all of the harms that our actions and inactions cause occur out of our sight. As a result, we regularly prioritize the smallest and most ephemeral benefits to ourselves over terrible outcomes or major lost opportunities for others—often unthinkingly, but sometimes with full awareness we are doing so.

Consider (as we did earlier) the value of the small, temporary enjoyment we might get from eating out at a nice restaurant against the value of other things that could be generated with that same amount of money, such as restoring vision to a person who has gone blind from cataracts. Or consider the value of the modest personal enjoyment an NGO's staffers might get from working five percent fewer hours (thirty-eight hours versus forty) against the value of their NGO helping five percent more children escape poverty or physical abuse. It's understandable that we might prioritize our small pleasures over someone else's small pleasures, and our major needs over someone else's major needs. But when we regularly weight ninety minutes of slightly increased personal enjoyment as more important than years of vision for someone else, when we regularly weight the comfort of a slightly more relaxed mental state for ourselves as more important than easing the suffering of someone in extreme misery, something must be off with the calibration of our ethical scales.

Addressing the fourth box is ultimately an exercise in recalibrating those scales. Once we do so, it is far easier to see the logic in—and have the willpower to—give up some of the fleeting enjoyments and comforts we are often so focused on procuring for ourselves in favor of bringing major benefits to those in great need.

Trade-offs for Others

Just as it's important to consider the trade-offs between benefits to ourselves and benefits to others, it's also important to consider the trade-offs that exist between doing good in one area and doing good in another area. When we act to help those in need, we are forced to decide which problems and outcomes we will prioritize and which we will neglect. In other words, we must choose who we will help and who we will ignore.

Consider the purchase of a box of cereal. Walk down the aisle of a natural foods store and you'll see a range of purported social benefits listed on the boxes of many cereal brands. Real examples include brands touting themselves as organic, woman-owned, vegan, veganic (which means the manure used to grow the crops did not contain animal byproducts), biodynamic, fair trade, non-GMO, using heirloom grains, bee-friendly, locally made, contributing a portion of proceeds to charity, and so on. A shopper that strives to be socially conscious and to do good in the world may think all or many of these attributes are valuable, and they might therefore aim to buy a brand that ticks as many of these boxes as possible—for example, a biodynamic, fair-trade, bee-friendly, locally made cereal brand. If they do, though, they are likely trading off those goods against something else: a low price.

Several of these socially conscious attributes add additional production costs. Further, the companies that try to address as many of these areas as possible are often small brands that lack economies of scale. As a result, our socially conscious shopper can expect to pay at least twice as much—and possibly three times as much—as they would have paid for a box of conventional cereal. Supporting the box-ticking brand might result in four dollars less in the shopper's pocket. And given we all have a limited amount of money, the decision to buy that brand of cereal is a decision not to use the marginal four dollars in another way, including donating it to an effective charity.

Our socially conscious shopper must therefore choose between two competing goods. They can financially support a business they think is doing things in a better way, or they can donate more money to a great charity. And in this case, the reality is that four dollars donated to an effective charity is likely to accomplish far, far more good in the world than spending an additional four dollars on a box of biodynamic, fair-trade, bee-friendly, locally made cereal. And while we are highlighting just two competing goods here, there are of course countless ways the four dollars could be used to do some good in the world, including giving it to different charities, using it for other types of responsible purchasing, investing it to make more money to later donate, and so on.

The cereal example is somewhat silly and has been exaggerated for effect, but it illustrates the fact that for everything we do, including actions we take to do good in the world, there is a trade-off of many other good things we don't do and are no longer able to do. Any time we are taking on some marginal cost to bring about something good, whether through a purchasing decision, donation to charity, political campaign contribution, expenditure decision (for those working at an NGO or socially impactful business), or so on, we should therefore consider the trade-off of what other good that money could have brought about if used in another way. The same is true for how we use our time and our mental energy.

Choosing between different goods with our money, time, and energy—choosing what to act on and what to ignore—can be tricky. It doesn't feel good to forgo doing something that in principle we think is a good thing to do (such as buying a more responsibly produced product) just because our marginal money or time can do more good if used a different way. It also doesn't feel nice, when we're trying to do something good, to be reminded that there are problems we are choosing to ignore and people we are choosing not to help. The notion that this is a deliberate decision we've made can feel unsettling.

For this reason, those who care about many different social issues and who see similarities or interplay between those issues will sometimes engage in issue-stacking: pursuing efforts that appear to address multiple social problems at once. My first real job after college was working at a project of the University of Pennsylvania that attempted to simultaneously address the issues of urban poverty, food deserts, poor eating habits, and lack of youth business skills. It did this primarily by running community vegetable gardens and produce stands, and doing related classroom education, in a low-income neighborhood. It was a very popular program, and one that received great press attention. It was also a program that achieved little change relative to the time, energy, and money invested. This was not because of poor planning, lack of funding, or lack of care; those that ran and worked for the program cared a lot. It is simply the case that while the problems of urban poverty, food deserts, poor eating habits, and lack of youth business skills have clear overlap, attempting to do charitable programming that addresses all four gives a very tiny range within which to work. The limited programming options that theoretically addressed all four areas were simply not effective at making meaningful progress in any area.

As another example, one may think animal suffering is an important problem to address and may also feel compelled to help refugees fleeing from warzones. But that doesn't mean donating to a nonprofit that helps refugees care for their pets, or that tries to help both refugees and animals simultaneously in some other fashion, is the best approach. We would do far more good for both animals and refugees by donating some money to the most effective animal protection charities and some money to the most effective interventions for helping refugees than we would by donating to a charity that worked to help both groups simultaneously.

If it's difficult to accept that we cannot effectively address numerous issues we care about simultaneously, and we must therefore choose what to prioritize and what to deprioritize or ignore completely, it can be even more challenging to deal honestly with the fact that two goods we value can sometimes be in direct competition with one another. Consider, for example, the (currently) competing goods of reducing extreme poverty in the world and reducing climate emissions and harm to animals.

People moving out of extreme poverty is a good, desirable outcome. A reduction in the likelihood of climate catastrophe is a good, desirable outcome. Animals being spared from lifelong suffering is a good, desirable outcome. Unfortunately, right now and for the foreseeable future, making progress in the first of these areas means causing harm in the second two. Global historical data makes crystal clear that as wealth and per capita GDP increase in a country, including in extremely low-income countries, carbon emissions and meat consumption (and with it the suffering of animals on factory farms) increase in a nearly linear correlation. As a result, one of these goods is in direct competition with the other two.

We certainly could imagine a way in which the world could achieve progress at eradicating global poverty without increasing climate emissions or causing more animals to suffer. But how things could theoretically be done, and how things have actually played out for the past fifty years and realistically will continue to play out for at least the next several decades, are two different things. For the foreseeable future, the good of poverty reduction will be odds with the goods of climate reduction and animal welfare.

There are countless other areas in which two or more real goods stand at odds with one another in a similar fashion. If we want to make real progress for those in need, we must deal honestly and deliberately with the reality that trade-offs like these present. We must recognize that not all good outcomes are of equal value; that certain goods will have negative repercussions in other areas and those repercussions are acceptable; and conversely that achieving some goods will have such negative percussions that it's actively harmful to pursue them, even if they are good in and of themselves.

A Final Word on Trade-offs

This chapter has focused on dealing honestly with trade-offs because many of us—including many who earnestly would like to make the world a better place—can be reluctant to acknowledge such trade-offs exist. Why would that be?

While there are likely multiple reasons, including some of the nonconscious biases touched on in this book, a primary reason we are reluctant to acknowledge trade-offs is probably the simple fact that it doesn't feel good. If a trade-off exists, it means that at the very least there is some group we care about that we are ignoring and leaving behind. In other cases, acknowledging trade-offs means accepting that when we are making progress in one area we care about, we are preventing progress or even causing active harm to some other group of individuals who we also care about. The thought that we are doing these things can cut sharply against the personal identity and self-perception of those who strive to be socially conscious and to do good in the world.

Acknowledging trade-offs also cuts sharply against the worldview many people have that goods in the world tend to all converge, such that all causes they consider to be socially beneficial dovetail with and bolster all other causes they also consider to be socially beneficial. Such social goods are good for everyone, other than perhaps a few rich corporate executives or corrupt politicians. Goods for one marginalized group or one social cause are also good for others.

The intuition many have that the world operates in this way may be related to what Daniel Kahneman has termed the Just World Fallacy, another one of his fifty-two well-documented human biases. The Just World Fallacy is the belief that people get what they deserve and that good things happen to good people. Perhaps by extension, our intuition might tell us that things that are good for us will be good for the world as well, and that things that are good for one group will be good for others too. Inaccurate perceptions that win-win solutions always exist when it comes to philanthropy, or to personal enjoyment versus doing good for others, and that we need not make tradeoffs, may stem in part from this universal human bias.

But probably the biggest reason some are inclined to deny the existence of trade-offs between their own enjoyment and the well-being of others is simple self-interested rationalization.

We want to be comfortable, and we want our lives to be enjoyable. Those who want to make the world a better place are no less likely than anyone else to rationalize their way toward decisions that make things more pleasant and comfortable for themselves, including when it comes to charitable efforts. The most typical approach for those who donate, volunteer, or work for charitable entities tends to be to try to do some good while staying within the bounds of what is relatively enjoyable.

It's understandable that anyone would take this approach. What is more human than to strive for personal comfort, security, and enjoyment? Yet if we want to own the fourth box, if we want to be high performers when it comes to reducing the suffering of others, this approach will not get us particularly far. An athlete who prioritizes pleasantness and avoids discomfort, who puts in no more than a moderate amount of effort and is unwilling to optimize their life toward the pursuit of their craft, will not get far and will never achieve their full potential.

Similarly, if we want to fully tackle the Good Things Not Yet Done and reach our own peak performance (or anything close to it), we need to accept that trade-offs exist and recognize and embrace the ones that allow us to do the most good, even when doing so is not pleasant. The mentality that got us interested in doing charitable work in the first place is likely a very different mentality from the one we need to cultivate in order to have the largest positive impact we can for the world.

CONCLUSION

Apathy and Action

> *"If you're going to try, go all the way. There is no other feeling like that. You will be alone with the gods, and the nights will flame with fire...it's the only good fight there is."*
> —CHARLES BUKOWSKI

This book, and many of its earlier chapters, started with a quote on the importance of taking action to help others in need and on our ethical culpability when we fail to do so. Quotes like these catch our attention because they capture sentiments that we believe have a great deal of truth but that we don't always keep in mind or act upon. Here is a final one-liner to add to that list: "The opposite of love is not hate; the opposite of love is apathy."

While this sentiment has been expressed many times and in varying ways, the first person I recall hearing it from and who I attribute it to in my own life is Charlie McCarthy, a Byzantine priest from New England. McCarthy's comment came in the middle of a roughly twelve-hour series of lectures he had delivered years earlier, and which I watched with rapt attention on a collection of crackling VHS tapes at the age of nineteen. While McCarthy, like Kierkegaard, spoke from a Christian perspective, his argument remains valid and reasonable regardless of one's personal religious beliefs: apathy is the opposite of love, and in some ways is even more condemnable than active hatred of those in need.

What does apathy look like from the outside? It is inaction. Failing to act to help those in great need is the textbook definition of apathy, of not caring. Inaction is apathy put into practice.

And if apathy in practice is inaction, then it stands to reason that love in practice is action. The feelings we refer to as "love" or "caring" in our everyday lives—the experience of a particular emotion sweeping through us or the conscious reflection on a particular belief we hold—are something else. Those feelings of love and caring, those internal political and social beliefs that we regard as demonstrations of the fact that we care, are in and of themselves largely irrelevant for others. In the world that exists beyond the borders of our brain, the world where other individuals live and experience joy and suffering, caring is an action. Love is an action. To love and to care mean to act, in service of the good of another.

This book has focused its discussion on the overlooked harms of inaction, but the flip side of that is the cheerier insight that love is action. This idea is also not a novel one. It has been expressed one way or another by most major world religions, shows up in literary classics and public speeches, and even adorns trite posters and throw pillows.

Yet like many quotable concepts, the idea that apathy is the opposite of love, and that apathy is inaction while love is action, likely feels foreign to our daily life, unintegrated into how we think about ourselves and the world, even if the words ring vaguely true. It's therefore an idea worth reflecting on. And if we agree with it, it's worth thinking through the implications that idea has for our own lives. This book has been an attempt to do just that.

Of course action and inaction, love and apathy, and caring and not caring are not binary ones and zeros. They are ends of a spectrum that we will always find ourselves somewhere between. None of us is constantly taking action or forever inactive, unrelentingly loving and caring for those who are suffering or constantly meeting others' suffering with apathy and a lack of concern. Since we will never find ourselves fully at either end of the spectrum, the practical questions for those of us who want to live ethically, who want to make the world a better place and improve the lives of others, are these: Where are we on the spectrum now, and where do we want to be? What standards of caring, of action, should we expect of ourselves and aspire to move closer toward?

Few people live most of the time at the fully apathetic end of the spectrum, not caring whatsoever about the suffering of others. And if you've spent the money and taken the time to read through a book about ethics like this one, it's likely you're not at the fully apathetic extreme yourself. But if we're honest with ourselves, most of us might conclude we're at a point on the spectrum we could call (perhaps a bit harshly) apathy adjacent. We care enough to take some action, but only within the bounds of what's comfortable for us. We don't act to the point of discomfort, or anywhere close to it. We don't give of our money, time, or mental energy to the point of real strain, or anywhere close to it.

To be more precise, this is where most of us stand on the spectrum when it comes to caring for and taking action to help others in the world who are in great need but who we don't know personally. In other areas of life, it is the norm to give and sacrifice heavily on behalf of others.

Consider, for example, the decision to raise a child. In the western world, raising a child costs hundreds of thousands of dollars, requires sacrificing a similarly vast number of hours (including enduring serious sleep deprivation early on), and—according to research—results in a very serious drop in our personal happiness for many years. Data shows that on average parents see their personal happiness drop to a lifetime low during their children's toddler years; they do not regain pre-parenthood levels of happiness until after their children have reached adulthood.

There are certainly some personal benefits to raising a child, such as the financial and emotional safety they provide for one's later years and the greater sense of meaning they can give to one's life. But the point is that parenthood is an area where those who adopt or have a child are—whether intentionally or unintentionally—choosing to give up a great deal of their time, money, and mental energy and to suffer a real drop in personal happiness, ostensibly for the sake of someone else. And parenting is just one example. There are many additional areas of life where similarly high levels of sacrifice are not only common but expected. We covered a number of these earlier, such as soldiers serving in the military and parents in developing economies working long hours in grueling conditions to give their children a better future.

But when it comes to the domain of charity, of working to help others we don't know who are enduring great suffering, this ethic is mostly absent. The amount of time, money, and energy we are willing to give, the amount of risk we are willing to take, and the hits (temporary or protracted) to our personal happiness that we are willing to endure are far smaller. The standards we hold ourselves to are far lower.

One reason for this, among others, may be the lack of good models. New parents have an endless number of other parents who have come before (including their own) who modeled for them the willingness to lose sleep, to accept harried and stressful days, and to deal with the emotional turmoil of raising children. Soldiers can look to friends and relatives who previously served, older soldiers in their unit, and the tens of millions of soldiers who have served before. Those working long hours in grueling conditions in order to escape extreme poverty and give their children a brighter future likely have many friends and family members around them doing the same thing.

Such models are rare in the world of charity. The number of individuals organizing and optimizing their life around a central goal of reducing as much suffering as they can is vanishingly low, and those who do are rarely publicly visible let alone celebrated. The publicly visible examples of charity that get celebrated, and thereby modeled for others to emulate, are quite different.

What is most often celebrated is the fact that a person or entity did anything at all to help others. There are an untold number of local (and occasionally some national) news stories about a Boy Scout troop, community group, child, company, or so on carrying out some well-intentioned charitable endeavor. Occasionally what is celebrated is a wealthy individual donating a particularly massive amount of money, even when such donations usually entail no personal sacrifice on the part of the giver. (In many cases, such as donations to universities, arts centers, hospitals, and similar institutions, such donations also have a fairly minimal positive impact on the world.) In recent years, the fact that a person or entity merely took a side on a social issue or made a public statement of support for an issue has become grounds for media or social media attention and public applause.

These are the models of charitable behavior that are on display for the average person to see, internalize, and copy in their own lives. There are certainly upsides to these sorts of stories: they model the idea that we should act to help others, give of our wealth, and speak out against harms and injustice. But their framing often sends the message that what matters, what is worth celebrating, is the mere act of doing anything that seems charitable. How much effort was put in, how thoughtfully it was done, and—most importantly—what the overall impact was, are nearly irrelevant in terms of what merits attention and praise.

It is the charity news equivalent to a newspaper sports section that covered all athletic endeavors at random, from a seven-year-old running across a field to a retiree hitting practice balls at a tennis club, without any focus on the best players, teams, and records in each sport. While there are probably benefits to writing about a variety of athletic pursuits, there is a major cost to not weighting attention toward results, and to not focusing attention on those who train, play and perform at the highest level.

Having publicly visible exemplars who put in significant physical and mental work, who sacrifice their time so significantly for their chosen pursuit, and who (as a result) have reached the highest levels of performance, inspires more people to do the same. Such exemplars provide a model to follow and a standard of performance to strive after, to meet, and ultimately to surpass. In the sports world, each generation of athletes is inspired by the icons of the prior generation whose example motivates them to work harder, longer, and smarter. In the charity world, the relative public absence of such models—people who are willing to significantly sacrifice their time, money, and mental energy to perform at a higher level—reduces the number of others who will choose to do the same in the future. It reduces the number of people who view such an approach as admirable or desirable in the first place.

It is with that in mind that much of this book has focused on the question of standards. On the spectrum of apathy to caring, of inaction to inaction, what standard should we hold ourselves to? What models should we look to as exemplars to try to emulate?

Embracing the fourth box, paying attention to the things we don't do, creates an impossible standard as a starting point, one which calls for ceaseless caring and ceaseless action—striving at all times to use our time, money, and mental energy in the ways that most reduce extreme suffering in the world. Since, of course, none of us will ever live up to that standard, the practical argument of this book is that we should set a much higher standard for ourselves than we currently have for what it looks like to be a good and caring person. Since such standards and the pursuit of such standards are not common in the charitable world, we looked to other sectors for role models. This included looking to elite athletics, the military, and other areas in which embracing a significant level of sacrifice, a significant level of discomfort, and a significant amount of optimizing one's life around a key central goal are the norm.

Be proud of the good things you have done for others before and that you are doing for others now. Try to avoid doing bad things that harm others. Be proud of the harms you're avoiding causing through conscious purchasing decisions or self-restraint. But most of all, pay attention to the good things you are not yet doing but could do. This is the area where each of us has the greatest ability to bring about the world we want to see. This is the area where each of us has the greatest ability to reduce extreme suffering in the world. In every area of current inaction—inaction with our time, with our money, with our mental energy—the potential for action and impact awaits.

A typical book might conclude here by wrapping things neatly into a win-win conclusion. It might apply the finishing bow by stating that if you take the path advocated for here, if you give more deeply of yourself to help others who are suffering greatly, it will make your life happier and more enriched.

Giving far more of our money, time and energy to help those in need certainly could have that effect. As discussed earlier, we are very poor predictors of what will add to or take away from our happiness. And in the tug of war between our desire for immediate pleasure and comfort and our desire for long-term happiness and meaning (the achieving of which often requires the denial of short-term pleasures), those who focus on the long term rarely regret it. How many elite athletes or parents who worked long hours at unpleasant jobs to create a better future for their children look back with regret on the sacrifice of time, money, and energy they made? How many wake up each morning feeling their lives are not or were not worth living? Not many. For all the short-term suffering and temporary reductions in happiness they bring about, life orientations such as these also provide a sense of purpose and direction, feelings of pride and well-being, and an empowering realization of what's possible when one is willing to embrace the uncomfortable.

So, it's entirely possible that the approach advocated for in this book could add to your overall happiness and enjoyment of life. But the book is not going to end on that message. Because while such an approach might ultimately make your life better, it also might not. It might have no discernible effect. It might make your life less enjoyable. Most likely, the long-term impact on your own personal happiness will probably be difficult to tell.

What we do know is that in the short term, the approach advocated for in the book is more likely to feel like it's taking away from your happiness than that it's adding to it. Much like the choice between broccoli and French fries, between hitting the gym for a workout and watching movies on the couch, the choice to give more of our resources to help those who are suffering often feels (in the moment) like a choice between enjoyment and sacrifice, between our own happiness and something else.

Most importantly of all, we are not going to end on a win-win message because increasing personal happiness is not the goal here. The goal of the approach advocated for in this book is reducing the amount of extreme suffering in the world. As discussed earlier, true win-wins are rare in life. Having more of one desirable outcome usually requires having less of another. There are clearly many situations—from parenthood to war to grueling working conditions for low-wage workers—where a decision must be made between the understandable desire for personal happiness and the desire to help others. To have more of one thing, we must tolerate having less of another. In at least some situations, using more of our time, money, and energy to help those in extreme suffering will require sacrificing a bit of our own personal happiness. That is life. Which of these two outcomes we will prioritize is a choice each of us faces minute to minute and day to day.

So, let's end instead with the following admonition. When making the choice between action and inaction in response to extreme suffering in the world, when making the choice to spend or not spend more of your resources to help those who are suffering, and when that choice feels in the moment like a choice between enjoyment and sacrifice, choose sacrifice nine times out of ten. Push harder. Expend more. Give and act not to the point of breaking but to the point of discomfort and strain. When you don't want to do it, do it anyway—not for your own benefit but because the extreme suffering of others is more important than your mild discomfort or loss of enjoyment.

In the end, it's as simple as that.

DEDICATION

After otherwise completing the book, I sat to write this dedication on a bench in front of the grave of Soren Kierkegaard in the bucolic Assistens Cemetery in Copenhagen, Denmark. Kierkegaard died at the age of forty-two, the same age I was the year I finished writing this book. He is buried in a family plot beneath a plain, weathered, and slightly tilted tombstone that is shaded by the drooping, willowy limbs of a several-hundred-year-old tree. Kierkegaard's name, birth date and date of death are engraved halfway down the stone, sitting discretely beneath those of his parents and another older relative whose name and details take top billing. It is an understated placement for a man who is considered by many to be the first existentialist philosopher and among the several dozen most prominent philosophers in history.

This book is dedicated with gratitude to Kierkegaard, one great ape whose thinking and writing—thoughts he pondered to himself walking the streets of the city and writing he scribbled by hand alone, sometimes to a positive public response and sometimes to public disdain—long after his death, taught another great ape a different and better way to think and act. While life is complex and there are a myriad of factors that shape us and our choices, it's clear that Kierkegaard's writings had a major impact on the trajectory of my life. They shifted my thoughts and beliefs and, consequently, my actions in a way that reduced or prevented the suffering of a significant number of individuals. (Most of these individuals are nonhuman animals, given my personal focus on animals due to their huge numbers, the intense misery they endure, and the cost-efficiency with which their suffering can be ameliorated.)

I wouldn't say his work has made my life a happier one; it's very hard to tell, but I don't think it has. Yet, as personally grateful as I am to those whose presence, friendship, kindness, support, discoveries, sacrifice, and work have clearly made my own life happier, I feel a unique debt of gratitude to those like Kierkegaard whose work has bent the arc of my life and my own use of time, money, and energy in a direction that reduced the suffering of others. To have the good fortune to be guided in that way by another person, to be bent in that way by their reasoning and writing, is a gift indeed. In the context of the comparatively easy and comparatively powerful lives most of us in the modern industrialized world live, the gift of that bending feels even more precious than the gifts that have made one's own life marginally or even meaningfully happier.

When I originally sat down to write this book, the first words of the introduction were "I don't think you're going to like this book." This was followed shortly thereafter by "And even if you do, I don't think you're likely to make significant changes from reading it." Those sentences were later replaced with a less dour approach. But I remain uncertain as to how much good will come from the time spent writing this book (other than the personal enjoyment of thinking through and expressing something I have personally believed so strongly for so long and that I virtually never see expressed in the world around me).

I hope that it does have some influence in bending you or others to do more for those in need. And sitting by Kierkegaard's grave, reflecting on the impact one regular, flawed, mortal individual can have on another and, more importantly, through them on the lives of those whose suffering is so deserving of our attention and intervention, gives me optimism and a flicker of existential peace. As is the case with all things in the world of living individuals, our ability to influence and impact the lives of others, and thereby create something of value outside ourselves, is so very, very, very, very finite—but also so very real.

Below his name and dates of birth and death, Kierkegaard's tombstone includes the following lines by the Danish psalmist Hans Adolph Brorson, translated here to English:

> There is but little time
> then I shall have won
> then all the strife
> will instantly have vanished
> then I can rest

There is indeed such little time for any of us. Let's see what we can win for those who suffer here in the land of the living, until we each reach our own final rest.

ABOUT THE AUTHOR

Nick Cooney is the founder and managing partner of venture capital firm Lever VC and the founder and board chair of Lever Foundation, a non-profit focused on advancing a humane and sustainable food system. He is the author of several previous books on effective charity and philanthropy work, including *How to Be Great at Doing Good: Why Results Are What Count and How Smart Charity Can Change the World* and *Change of Heart: What Psychology Can Teach Us About Spreading Social Change*. Cooney advises on effective giving and previously founded and co-founded the non-profits The Humane League and the Good Food Institute. A graduate of Hofstra University, he lives in the greater New York City region.